Guyana Emergent
The Post-Independence Struggle
for Nondependent Development

Robert H. Manley

Guyana Emergent
The Post-Independence Struggle for Nondependent Development

G. K. Hall & Co.   Boston, Massachusetts

Schenkman Publishing Co.   Cambridge, Massachusetts

Copyright © 1979 by Schenkman Publishing Co.

Library of Congress Cataloging in Publication Data

Manley, Robert H.   1927-
  Guyana emergent.

  Includes index.
  1. Guyana—Politics and government—1966-
I. Title.
F2385.M36   320.9'88'103   79-4190
ISBN 0-8161-9001-1

This publication is printed on permanent/durable acid-free paper
MANUFACTURED IN THE UNITED STATES OF AMERICA

To the People of Guyana,

who have struggled against much,

learned much in the struggle,

and taught me much.

Contents

PREFACE	ix
CHAPTER ONE From Slave Colony to Independence	1
CHAPTER TWO Political Leadership for the New Nation	19
CHAPTER THREE Enhancing Regional Ties	28
CHAPTER FOUR Obtaining Territorial Control	41
CHAPTER FIVE From Western Alignment to Nonalignment	55
CHAPTER SIX Toward Nondependent Development	72
CHAPTER SEVEN Identity in Transition	85
CHAPTER EIGHT Beyond the First Post-independence Decade	115
APPENDIX List of Interviews	117
NOTES	120
INDEX	153
ABOUT THE AUTHOR	159

Preface

When Guyana achieved political independence in May 1966 it could hardly be regarded as an autonomous actor in the world. Like many other new nations, it remained dependent on its former colonial master and on other nations in key economic, political and social aspects. Considered here are the strategies pursued during the country's first post-independence decade by its political leadership for transition from dependence and for achieving, maintaining or enhancing their own power. Also considered is the dramatic role Guyana has played in Caribbean integration and in leading, especially among Commonwealth nations of that region, decolonization and other aspects of ideological re-orientation.

During the ten-year period in question (1966-76) I made eight research trips to Guyana. The first was at the time of independence, the most recent at the time of the tenth anniversary observances, May 1976. Other research was conducted in Guyana in May 1967, December-January 1968-69 (at the time of the first post-independence national elections and of the uprising in the Rupinuni area of the country), December-January 1969-70, February 1970 (when conversion to Cooperative Republic status took place), July 1971 (during finalization of arrangements for nationalization of Aluminum Company of Canada holdings) and November 1973 (shortly after the second post-independence national elections). Other interviews and research were conducted while I was in Puerto Rico and other Caribbean areas and in the United States.

My debts for assistance over the years are many. Work proceeded while I was a faculty member at the Spelman College, The Atlanta University Center, the University of Puerto Rico at Rio Piedras, the Medgar Evers College of the City University of New York and at Seton Hall University. I wish to thank my colleagues at these institutions for their assistance. Special financial support was received from the Institute of Caribbean Studies, University of Puerto Rico, where I was based from August 1968 to August 1971, and from the Faculty Research Council, Seton Hall University.

In Guyana, the list of those who have helped with advice and counsel is long.

A number of colleagues at the University of Guyana are in this group, among them political scientist Harold Lutchman, economist Clive Thomas and historian Robert Moore. Eileen Cox, editor of the parliamentary record (Hansard), assisted greatly in locating materials. S.S. Ramphal, Rashleigh Jackson and Lloyd Searwar of the Ministry of External Affairs were unfailing in their willingness to provide insights and information. Frank Pilgrim assisted in many ways in his role with the Prime Minister's Office. Dr. Cheddi Jagan, Janet Jagan and others at the People's Progressive Party headquarters were always responsive to requests for information. Further indications of support in Guyana can be ascertained from the list of interviews, but even this fails to name a number of persons whose help was vital.

Caribbean scholars Herbert Addo, Robert Andersen, Fuat Andic, Carmen Gautier, J. Edward Greene, Harmannus Hoetink, Basil Ince, Gordon Lewis, Neville Linton, Milton Pabon, and Luis Vega gave important advice and assistance. At the Graduate School of Public Affairs, State University of New York at Albany, Theodore P. Wright, Jr. as well as Carlos Astiz, L. Gray Cowan, Michael Moss, Robert Rienow and Fred Tickner provided vital commentary and critique. Philip Singer, formerly of the Albany Medical School, was most helpful in sharing his knowledge about Guyana at the work's inception. Colette Mercier Amoda, Marie Weber Manley and Doris B. Sura provided outstanding assistance in preparing the manuscript. Susan Hughes, with usual outstanding skill, prepared the index, Katherine Diamond of G. K. Hall made important contributions as production editor. Finally, in addition to acknowledging vital assistance from my mother, brother and sister, I note valuable commentary at early stages of research design by Richard Falk, Charles Kindleberger, James Rosenau and the late Quincy Wright. I hope that the result is worthy of the interest and commitment of those mentioned and unmentioned, without whose effort this work would not have been possible.

October 1978   RHM

Chapter 1

From Slave Colony to Independence

It may be that in no other nation in the contemporary world is there as much political consciousness per capita as in Guyana.[1] Having known over an extended period the travails of colonization, both Dutch and British, comprised as it is of peoples of diverse cultural backgrounds, having gone through intense ideological struggles, with relatively high literacy, and with the bulk of the population living along a coastal belt, thus facilitating intensive communication, Guyana has had the ingredients for political sophistication and it has utilized the ingredients.[2]

Though small in population (approximately 680,000 as of independence, May 1966, some 800,000 a decade later), Guyana has emerged dramatically into the world political stage, expressing an impatience with subjugation and dependency, increasingly allying itself with and adding to forces striving for a new system in which developing nations would have a more just status. The present lack of docility is consistent with a history in which the spirit of resistance to oppression has flourished. The Amerindians of the area were able to avoid either extermination or enslavement at the hands of the Europeans. The first major slave revolt in the New World took place on the nation's soil (Berbice, 1763). Guyana's mass movement for independence and decolonization so unrelentingly insisted on change that the British government in 1953 declared a state of emergency, suspended the constitution and landed troops. It is striking too, and perhaps indicative of political maturity and stability of the population, that during the entire turbulent period from 1950 to the late 1970's, the two leading figures in politics have been Cheddi Jagan and Forbes Burnham. Working in uneasy alliance in the early 1950's and to an extent from the mid-1970's onward, Jagan was the senior partner during the earlier period, and in the more recent years Burnham has had top leadership.

Guyana's two largest ethnic groups are the East Indians, which as of independence in 1966 were estimated to constitute 50.71% of the population, and Africans, then estimated at 30.81%. Estimates for other groups were: Mixed, 12.08%, Amerindians, 4.66%, Portuguese .91%, Chinese .62%, and non-Portuguese Europeans .21%.[3] The annual growth of population was in the range of 2 1/2% as of 1975, with a distribution according to sex of 51% female, 49% male.[4]

The bulk of the non-Amerindian population has historically been concentrated along the nation's coast and up the major rivers for some twenty miles. The interior, with the exception of bauxite mining areas such as Wizmar-MacKenzie (now known as Linden), is thinly settled, and overall, the country, with 83,000 square miles, has a population density of only some 9.5 per square mile (based on the 1975 population estimates). The Portuguese, Chinese, non-Portuguese European, and mixed populations were as of 1960 predominantly urban. The percentage of Africans living in urban centers increased from 26.4% in 1891 to 43.3% in 1960. Likewise, the percentage of East Indians in urban centers went from 5% in 1891 to 13.4% in 1960.[5]

The original Amerindian settlers consisted of a number of tribes inhabiting an area now comprised of parts of Venezuela, Brazil, and the three Guianas.[6] Lying between areas explored and eventually settled by the Spanish and the Portuguese, the Guianas (the name was used by the Amerindians, meaning "land of many waters") were explored and settled by the British, Dutch, and French, including Sir Walter Raleigh in search of the elusive "El Dorado."

The first European settlement of permanence appears to have been in 1616, by a group of Dutch and English settlers under Dutch leadership. Known as Kyk-over-al, it was located on an island some forty miles up the broad-mouthed Essequibo River at its confluence with the Cuyuni and Mazaruni rivers and not far from the present town of Bartica.[7] A charter authorizing settlement of the Guiana coast was granted by the Dutch States General to the Dutch West Indies Company in 1621. After initial trading with the Amerindians in dyes, hemp, wood, and tobacco, sugar and tobacco plantations were developed in the areas of the Essequibo, Demerara, and Berbice rivers. Not only Dutch, but British and other Europeans settled in the area. Slaves were brought from Africa (and from islands in the Caribbean to which they had already been taken by Europeans) and soon the African population outnumbered the Europeans.[8] Peter Newman notes that: "By 1760 the British were more numerous than the Dutch in Demerara (and of course Negroes far more numerous than either)."[9]

A brief historical account published by the British Government in 1966 states that

> after 1746, when settlement was invited in the Demerara region also, plantations were rapidly established along the river. Englishmen from Barbados were among the settlers attracted to the area by grants of land and tax concessions, many of them bringing their slaves with them.[10]

Colin Henfrey comments:

> Private tobacco and sugar plantations followed the trading posts, spreading into the neighboring regions of Demerara and Berbice. These soon created a Caribbean rather than Latin American system of the small European plantocracy, vastly outnumbered by its slaves, which was to be the backbone of Guianese development.[11]

Slave revolts occurred throughout the Caribbean area during the eighteenth century, culminating in the successful uprising in Haiti which ended French domination there (1791-1803). What was perhaps the earliest major Caribbean revolt took place in the Berbice area of Guiana in February 1763. The Dutch were expelled from a substantial portion of the Berbice Colony and were forced to enter into negotiations with the slaves, whose leader, Cuffy, was referred to as "Governor" in communications from the rebels to the Dutch. However, eventually Dutch troop reinforcements arrived in the area, and within about a year the Dutch had re-established control. Cuffy took his own life during the rebellion. The surviving revolt leaders were savagely tortured and were executed by the Dutch after they regained control. The beginning date of the revolt, February 23, was commemorated by its utilization as the date upon which Guyana became a Cooperative Republic in 1970. Cuffy is now eulogized as a National Hero.[12]

The Dutch were paramount in the area now known as Guyana until the Anglo-Dutch War of 1781, after which Guiana changed hands several times. The British remained in control from 1803 onward, however, and in 1814 the colonies of Demerara, Essequibo, and Berbice were ceded by the Netherlands to Great Britain. These territories were united as the Colony of British Guiana in 1831, with the capital established at Stabroek, at the mouth of the Demerara River, renamed by the British "Georgetown."[13] The Colony of Berbice had been administered by the Dutch somewhat separately from those of Essequibo and Demerara, which were closely related in administration. The Dutch continued with their holdings in what is now known as Surinam. These holdings had been ceded to them by the British at the Treaty of Breda, 1667, in exchange for Dutch interests in what is now New York State.

The slave trade was abolished as a legal practice in 1807 and slavery itself abolished in 1834, although a four-year transitional period of apprenticeship or "semi-slavery" continued until August 1, 1838. Africans more and more left the plantations, often to work small holdings they acquired, and the plantation owners sought other sources of labor, bringing Portuguese from Madeira, a few immigrants from England, Germany, and Scotland, and, commencing in 1838, indentured labor from India. Some 238,960 Indians arrived between 1838 and 1917, when the indenture system was terminated. Chinese labor was

4 Guyana Emergent

also utilized. According to figures utilized by Raymond Smith, 31,628 Portuguese came from Madeira, the Azores, and Cape Verde from 1835 to 1882; 42,562 persons from the West Indies (presumably mostly originally from Africa) between 1835 and 1928; 13,355 from Africa from 1838 to 1865; 14,189 Chinese from 1855 to 1912 (the bulk before 1866); 208 persons from Malta in 1839; and seventy from the United States in 1840.[14] A substantial number of Indians exercised their right of repatriation and returned to India. Dwarka Nath asserts that from 1843 to 1955, 75,792 sailed for India on immigrant ships.[15]

The British had taken over relatively intact the Dutch constitutional system for the area, operating with a Governor appointed from London and a combination of appointed and elected representatives in various decision-making bodies.[16] Property requirements for voting and for holding office effectively barred the former slaves and the newly arrived East Indians until constitutional reforms of 1891 extended the franchise to an extent. It has been estimated that in 1850-51, when total population was about 127,000, the electorate consisted of 916 persons, almost all of whom were Europeans. By 1910 the number had increased to 4,104, a still not-overly-generous number considering that the population was now about 303,000.[17] As of 1915, British, Portuguese, and Chinese segments of the population were heavily overrepresented in the electorate and Africans fared better than East Indians.[18]

In 1928, constitutional changes were effected, bringing the political system into conformity with other British West Indies politics (aside from Barbados) under the so-called Crown Colony System. The powers of the Governor and, standing behind him, the Colonial Office were changed, with officials of the Government (Attorney General, etc.) and the Governor's appointees a majority in the thirty-man Legislative Council and twelve-man Executive Council. Whites (presumably mostly British) dominated both bodies, at least as initially constituted. Fourteen of the thirty Legislative Council members were elected, the remainder being either officials of the Government or nominees of the Governor. The Executive Council was constituted wholly of officials of the Government and nominees of the Governor, with the proviso that two of the Governor's nominees were to be elected members of the Legislative Council. Vere T. Daly views the 1928 constitutional changes as marking "a step backward" and as "a defeat for the Guianese People."[19] The framework inherited from the Dutch had its defects, he asserts, but could have been used effectively by a majority party to govern the country. Utilization of the Crown Colony System is seen as another phase in the "struggle for political and economic influence between European planter interests, and the Negro, coloured, Portuguese and, more latterly, Indian professionals and commercial classes" with the planters recapturing in 1928 some of the political ground lost since the last previous major changes in the colony's governing structure, in

1891. However, Daly does note that under the 1928 alterations, women were admitted into the franchise and elected members of the Legislative Council introduced into the Executive.[20]

The 1930's were a period of unrest in the British West Indies, where the world-wide depression was harshly felt. Strikes and riots, starting in 1934, spread in the area, including British Guiana. Throughout the area the trade union movement grew in strength and larger segments of the populations, impelled by the dire circumstances, questioned the colonial conditions in which they found themselves. Following serious disorders in Guiana and Jamaica in June 1938, the Colonial Office was moved, in August of that year, to provide for the appointment of a Royal Commission, under the chairmanship of Lord Moyne, "to investigate social and economic conditions in all the West Indian territories and to make recommendations."[21]

The Moyne Commission traveled throughout the area for fifteen months, taking testimony from hundreds of individuals and groups. A long and comprehensive report of the commissioners described the plight of the populations, the unemployment, malnutrition, ill-health, and inadequacies of education.[22] Written in the first months of the Second World War, only the recommendations of the report were published at the time, the detailed survey of conditions not being made public until 1945. Its recommendations, calling for greater involvement of local people in government and administration and extension of the franchise, constituted a water-shed in the life of British Guiana and the other British West Indies colonies. In terms of constitutional changes, first implementations of the report came in British Guiana in 1943 and 1945 with the reduction of property qualifications for candidates for the Legislative Council, reduction of property or income qualifications for voters and increasing the number of elected members to give them a majority in the Legislative Council.[23]

The stage was now set for the turbulent period of those decades in which Guyana found vigorous local leadership, well-organized political party life, and intensive ideological thrust, made the transition from colony to independent nation-state (1966) and then to status as a Cooperative Republic, the first nation so styled (1970), nationalized the major foreign-owned economic enterprises operating there, and became a moving force in the non-aligned nations group, hosting its foreign ministers conference in August 1972 and serving as a member of the group's central "bureau."

The leadership came initially in the person of Cheddi Jagan, East Indian son of a sugar estate "driver" (foreman of a gang) who, following his education as a dentist in the United States, returned to Guiana with his American-born wife Janet in December 1943. The Jagans became active in the political life of the Colony almost immediately and in the 1947 elections Dr. Jagan was elected to the Legislative Council, at the age of 29. In 1950 they were joined by a young

African barrister, Forbes Burnham, on his return from England where he had studied as a "Guiana Scholar," a scholarship awarded annually to the top student in the colony. With other emerging leaders of the period, they formed the People's Progressive Party (PPP), a party which following its split in 1955 became the basis for the two currently dominant parties, Jagan's People's Progressive Party (PPP) and Burnham's People's National Congress (PNC). Both factions resulting from the split operated under the name People's Progressive Party, a somewhat confusing state of affairs, until after the 1957 elections, when the Burnham-led group was restyled as the People's National Congress. The choice of party name may have reflected a desire for identity in voters' minds both with the already successful People's National Movement party in Trinidad, led by Dr. Eric Williams, and with the ruling Congress party in India.

A sweeping victory in April 1953 in the first elections held under universal adult suffrage (introduced with other constitutional changes that year) gave the PPP eighteen of twenty-four seats in the House of Assembly, which under the new constitution replaced the Legislative Council. However, as previously noted, in October 1953 the British Government suspended the new constitution. An appointed Legislative Council replaced the House of Assembly.

In a report of the British Guiana Constitution Commission under the chairmanship of Sir James Robertson, which was appointed to visit Guyana and recommend constitutional changes following the constitutional suspension, Dr. and Mrs. Jagan and several other PPP leaders were referred to as accepting "unreservedly the 'classical' communist doctrines of Marx and Lenin." On the other hand, Mr. Burnham and two other party leaders were classified as "socialists," with the assertion that "They were as bitterly opposed as their communist colleagues to British colonial rule, but they were not communists."[24] The suspension has been criticized by Raymond Smith as largely related to cold war circumstances,[25] and by Leo Despres on the ground that the charges of attempted communist takeover were not substantiated or in fact were without valid basis.[26] Vere T. Daly, while noting the cold war atmosphere of the period as a factor in the British action, is also of the opinion that "the P.P.P. ministers in seeking to implement their socialist election program were in effect embarking on a policy of confrontation and opposition to the Governor and his officials which was bound to lead to a breakdown of the fragile transitional constitution under which British Guiana was governed."[27]

Elections were again permitted in 1957, with the Jagan PPP group winning nine of fourteen elected seats in a newly established Legislative Council. Burnham's PPP group won three seats and two other parties one seat each. Following the 1957 elections Jagan began pushing in earnest for independence. The British were not ready to set any date for that event but did agree, under a new constitution put in effect after the 1961 elections, to internal self-government.

In elections of August 1961, Jagan's PPP was again victorious, winning twenty of the thirty-five seats in the Legislative Assembly provided for in the current constitution. Burnham's People's National Congress won eleven seats, and the United Force (UF), a party led by Portuguese businessman Peter d'Aguiar which had been formed in 1960, four seats.

The 1961-64 period was one of considerable ethnic and ideological conflict. Following the 1961 elections and the Jagan PPP victory, tensions in the country escalated at a dramatic rate, the assumption held by many apparently being that independence was near at hand and the country's future, whether seen in terms of ethnic domination or ideological thrust, or both, was in the balance. One group from the African community, led by Sidney King (now Eusi Kwayana) and H.H. Nicholson, known as the "Society for Racial Equality," went so far as to advocate partition of the country into an African zone, an East Indian zone, and a free zone.[28]

In February 1962, following presentation by the Jagan government of a proposed budget involving new and increased taxes and introduction by the PPP leadership of a resolution to set up a constitutional committee in preparation for a London conference in relation to independence, a protest demonstration, led by Burnham and d'Aguiar, which eventually involved some 60,000 persons, was held in Georgetown. Rioting ensued and in the extensive fires that resulted much of the heart of Georgetown was destroyed, with losses estimated at almost $11.5 million (West Indian). In the violence, eighty persons were injured and five killed, including thirty-nine police injured and one killed.[29]

In April 1963 a general strike, which lasted eighty days and paralyzed most of the country's import-export trade, ensued, with attendant injuries and property damage. Partly at issue was a PPP proposal for labor legislation, which Jagan defended as modeled on the U.S. Wagner Act. However, it seems clear that as matters developed, the strike became a test of strength between competing ideological and ethnic factions, played out against a cold war background. United States unions, apparently backed by CIA funds, helped finance local unions supporting the strike. The strike ended in early July when the PPP withdrew the proposed labor legislation.[30]

Sir Harold Mitchell has commented:

> The widespread publicity given to the General Strike underlined the international importance attached to the struggle. To the United States, deeply disturbed by Cuban events, a Communist Guyana, which had frontiers with both Brazil and Venezuela, presaged

further danger. The country was far too near the approaches to the Orinoco, an important iron-ore route, for the Americans to be indifferent. Venezuela was grappling with Communist problems and stood out as a target for Castro's Cuba

The International angle to the Guyana crisis was also emphasized by advice to the striking unions from their U.S. counterparts and by aid which may have amounted to $80,000 a week. Creole fear that they might be exchanging British rule for another foreign ideology was matched by East Indian fears of Negro rule from Georgetown.[31]

In early 1964 violence again erupted after the Guiana Agricultural Workers Union, a sugar workers union affiliated with the PPP which sought to replace the Manpower Citizens Association as the major sugar union, called a strike. Disturbances were widespread, not only in the sugar-producing areas but in various villages and towns, and ethnic aspects of conflict were all too apparent. Vere T. Daly asserts that in the incidents of 1964 "176 persons were killed, 920 injured, 1,400 homes destroyed by fire, and about 15,000 persons forced to move their houses from one district to another in order to settle in communities where people of their own ethnic group predominated."[32]

In the meantime, at a Constitutional Conference held in London in October of 1963, a new general election was set, with no firm date established for independence. In both the 1963 Constitutional Conference and one held in the fall of 1962, Burnham and d'Aguiar had insisted that a system of proportional representation should be adopted and that elections should be held before independence. They pointed out that under the existing "first past the post" system, involving single member districts, Jagan's PPP had gained seats in numbers out of proportion to its percentage of the national vote. (In 1957 Jagan's PPP had won nine of fourteen seats with 47.5% of the total vote and in 1961 it won twenty of thirty-five seats with 42.6% of total vote.) Jagan, on the other hand, proposed retaining the single-member district system, reducing the voting age to eighteen, a move favorable to the PPP in view of the large proportion of East Indians in the younger age groups, and granting independence before elections. Unable to agree on these points of contention, the three leaders signed a letter to Mr. Duncan Sandys, the Colonial Secretary, dated October 25, 1963, which concluded, ". . . we are agreed to ask the British Government to settle on their authority all outstanding constitutional issues and we undertake to accept these decisions."[33]

Sandys' report, issued a few days later, favored proportional representation and did not lower the voting age from twenty-one. No firm date for independence was established, Sandys' report stating, "After the elections are over, the British Government will convene a conference to settle any remaining constitutional issues, and to fix a date for independence."[34] As to proportional representation, Sandys stated:

> The supporters of this system claim that since no one race constitutes a majority of the electorate, all parties will have to appeal for support to all races. In practice I doubt whether either the Indian or the African party could, under its present leadership, hope to increase appreciably its following among the other racial groups. On the other hand, I am satisfied that there is validity in the argument that in present circumstances, where no party commands an overall majority of votes, proportional representation would be likely to result in the formation of a coalition government of parties supported by different races, and that this would go some way towards reducing the present tension.[35]

With regard to voting age, Sandys asserted, "No case has been made to show that a lowering of the voting age would help to solve the problems which face British Guiana. I do not therefore propose to make any change."[36]

In the elections held in December 1964 under a proportional representation system in which all single member districts were abolished and each party was to receive the number of seats in the newly constituted fifty-three seat House of Assembly that its proportion of total national vote dictated, the PPP received 45.88% of the vote, for which it got twenty-four seats, the PNC 40.5% and twenty-two seats, and the United Force 12.41% and seven seats. The PNC and UF now formed a coalition government, with Burnham as Premier and d'Aguiar as Minister of Finance.

The independence constitutional conference was finally held in November 1965, but the PPP refused to participate, asserting that it could not do so until revocation of emergency orders (invoked by the Governor during rioting, when Jagan was Premier, and continued in effect by the Burnham-led government) under which several PPP supporters were being held without trial and until "other relevant matters, such as fundamental rights, and the necessity for achieving some broad political settlement" had been resolved.[37]

The conference resulted in establishment of May 26, 1966 as the date for independence. Under the independence constitution, voting age was to remain at twenty-one; proportional representation, with a fifty-three seat Parliament, was to continue; the current parliament was to have a term of not more than four years (meaning elections would have to be held again by December 1968); and thereafter Parliament was to have terms of not more than five years. The new nation would be a monarchy, with a Governor General appointed by the Queen, but at any time after January 1, 1969 (meaning after the next general election) it could become a republic by simple majority vote of its parliament.

Provisions safeguarding fundamental rights and freedoms of the individual were to be incorporated in the constitution. Certain provisions of the constitution were to be "entrenched" and would require for amendment, in the case of some provisions, approval by a majority of the electorate voting in a referendum, and in the case of others, a two-thirds majority of all members of parliament.[38]

As independence approached, Guyana continued to suffer the economic and social afflictions of many "developing" nations. According to a survey conducted by a United Nations expert, 21% of the labor force was unemployed in 1965. Underemployment was higher yet, according to the same survey, with approximately one-third of employed labor force working six months or less during the year.[39] School, sanitation, hospital, and housing facilities, while substantially better than in a number of third world countries, were surely inadequate for a significant portion of the population.

The bauxite industry continued to be entirely foreign-owned (Aluminum Company of Canada and Reynolds Aluminum) and in some minds British Guiana was still thought of interchangeably with Bookers' Guiana, after the British company owning the bulk of sugar lands and mills as well as heavily involved in shipping, import-export trade, insurance, retail trade, printing, and various other lines of endeavor. British, Canadian, American, and Indian companies controlled all commercial banking.[40]

Further, Venezuela was pressing more insistently, as independence neared, its claim to some five-eighths of Guyana's territory—everything west of the Essequibo River. Surinam, in 1962, the same year that Venezuela had begun to re-assert its claim in earnest, had revived a long-standing claim to a portion (much smaller than that claimed by Venezuela, involving some 7,000 square miles, as contrasted with approximately 50,000 claimed by Venezuela) lying to its south-west and Guyana's south-east, known as the "New River Triangle."

Guyana had not been a participant in the ill-fated West Indies Federation (1957-1962), but shortly after he became Premier (and even before independence), Burnham pushed for closer ties with other Commonwealth Caribbean polities. Within two years after independence, a new framework for regional integration, CARIFTA (Caribbean Free Trade Area), had been established and shortly thereafter the secretariat for the Commonwealth Caribbean Organization, CARIFTA's executive body, was headquartered in Georgetown. Another key element of the new regional integration bid, the Caribbean Development Bank, came into being in early 1970 and thereafter established its headquarters in Barbados. Then, on July 4, 1973, CARIFTA was transformed into CARICOM, the Caribbean Community, by execution at Chaguaramas, Trinidad, of a treaty providing for establishment of a common market, for coordination of foreign policies and enhancing efforts in functional cooperation in a broad range of areas.

With independence Guyana became a member of the Commonwealth of Nations and, at the first meeting of the United Nations General Assembly following independence (September 20, 1966), was accepted into UN membership. She maintained initially overseas missions only in London, New York (her permanent mission to the United Nations as well as a Consulate), Ottawa and Washington. Later, she opened missions in Caracas, Havana, Lusaka (Zambia), Kingston (Jamaica), New Delhi, Paramaribo (Surinam), Peking, and Rio de Janeiro.[41]

As previously noted, the life of the parliament elected in December 1964 was, under the independence constitution, not over four years. The People's Nation Congress-United Force coalition continued until shortly before the next election, which was called for December 16, 1968. Under legislation adopted in 1968, Guyanese citizens residing overseas were permitted to vote. According to announced results, the PNC received 55.81% of the vote, taking thirty of the fifty-three seats in Parliament, the PPP 36.49%, obtaining nineteen seats, and the United Force 7.41% and four seats. A fourth party, the Guyana United Muslim Party, fielded candidates in the election but it received only a fraction of one percent of the vote and no seats. The power of party leaders had been strengthened prior to the 1968 election by regulations calling for submission of slates of candidates for the fifty-three seats in alphabetical order. Following announcement of the vote, each party leader was to select from his party's slate a list of persons to serve in Parliament, corresponding to the number of seats the party was reported to have won. Under regulations prevailing for the 1964 election, candidate lists were presented in numerical order, with determination as to which candidates received seats based on position in this list.

There is ample reason to conclude that the results of the 1968 election were manipulated by various strategems, involving both internal and overseas voting, to provide a winning margin for the People's National Congress. In regard to internal voting, abuse of proxy voting and miscounting of ballots were probably the two most widespread practices distorting the results. The practice of proxy voting had been criticized by the Commonwealth Team of Observers for the 1964 elections as "liable to abuse,"[42] and there were reports of proxies obtained under duress and perhaps in some cases by outright fraud on behalf of the PNC in the 1968 elections. Scrutiny of the counting of ballots was made difficult, if not impossible, by the consolidation of counting in three locations in Georgetown, one in New Amsterdam, and one in Suddie, Pomeroon. The ballot boxes were transported long distances before counting took place and in the ensuing delays it was not possible for opposition parties to maintain scrutiny.

I was in Guyana at the time of the elections and was advised in the course of an interview with a leading figure of the United Force Party who attempted to scrutinize the counting procedure at one of the Georgetown locations, that he found stacks of ballots which had been classified as "all PNC," in which votes for other parties were interspersed. He reported that, in the confusion of handling counting from a number of election districts in the same place, it was impossible to maintain meaningful oversight of the counting procedures. Two PPP agents were reported to have found four bundles of ballot papers rubber-banded together in one ballot box in the Pomeroon District.[43]

As to overseas voting, the *Sunday Times* (London) reported that whereas the Ministry of Home Affairs of the Guyana Government had announced in August 1968 that there were 43,000 names on the registration list for Britain, statistics compiled by the British Home Office and the Institute of Race Relations in London "suggest that the maximum number of Guyanese over 21 (the voting age) is 23,000." The *Times* acknowledged that no completely accurate figures for Guyanese nationals in Britain existed.[44] Granada Television of Great Britain carried two films making strong allegations as to untrustworthiness of vote figures so obtained. Voter registrations in Britain and the United States were asserted to be grossly inflated, with only 4,700 of the 11,750 registered in the United States and 13,050 of the 44,301 registered in the United Kingdom viewed as genuine.[45] The *New York Times* correspondent who covered the 1968 election from Georgetown, Henry Giniger, reported that "Anti-Jaganites made it candidly clear before the election that any electoral method was legitimate to keep the devil away from the door."[46]

Almost immediately on the heels of the election, on January 2, 1969, a revolt of ranchers, aided by Amerindians, ensued in the Rupununi area of Guyana, deep in the interior, near the Brazil border but within territory claimed by Venezuela. Several Guyanese police were killed and the settlement of Lethem and two other settlements taken over, but Guyanese forces, rushed to the area, re-established control within a short time; a number of those involved in the revolt were captured, with others fleeing to Brazil and Venezuela. There were indications that the Venezuelan government had provided training and equipment for those involved in the revolt.[47]

No longer in harness with the more conservative United Force Party, Burnham soon announced that Guyana would be transformed into a Republic—a Cooperative Republic, the first nation so styled. Guyana was to achieve socialism through cooperativism.[48] Necessary legislation providing for the transition was enacted in August 1969, with the PPP giving its support and the United Force withholding its backing. The date for the conversion, February 23, 1970, was chosen to mark the anniversary of the initiation of the Berbice Slave Revolt of 1763. Cuffy, a leader of the revolt, was declared a national hero. The conversion took place as scheduled and at the same time the Cooperative National Bank, the first indigenous commercial banking institution in the country, was opened in newly constructed quarters in downtown

Georgetown.

With the British queen no longer symbolic head of state, the office of Governor General, in theory the Queen's local representative, was abolished and replaced by that of Republic President. Arthur Chung, a judge of the Guyanese Supreme Court, was elected by the National Assembly to serve a six-year term as the nation's first president. He was re-elected to a second six-year term in March 1976. Meaningful political power continued under the new arrangement to be exercised by the prime minister, with the presidency a largely symbolic and ceremonial role.

The year of conversion to Cooperative Republic status also saw the Venezuela and Surinam border disputes settled, at least on a temporary basis. In June 1970 agreement was reached with Venezuela under which for a minimum of twelve years that country would not claim sovereignty over the disputed territory and Guyana would not assert a claim to Venezuelan territory. In April of that year Prime Minister Burnham and Surinam's Minister-President, Dr. Jules Sedney, had agreed in principle to peaceful resolution of their countries' dispute. Procedures calling for immediate demilitarization of the affected region and for joint on-going discussions to assure cooperative relations were formalized in June.

Little more than a year after conversion to Cooperative Republic status, a decisive step toward national control over externally owned elements of the economy was taken with nationalization, effective July 1971, of the nation's largest bauxite mining and processing operation, Demerara Bauxite Company, Ltd., a wholly owned subsidiary of the Aluminum Company of Canada (ALCAN). Assets of the one other bauxite operation in the country, Reynolds (Guyana) Mines, a subsidiary of the United States company Reynolds Metals, were nationalized as of January 1975. In May of that year sugar lands and other assets of the British-owned Jessel Securities Ltd. were taken over.

The largest move toward control of foreign-owned resources was formalized at the time of the nation's tenth anniversary of independence, May 1976, with nationalization of all assets in Guyana of Booker McConnell Ltd., a United Kingdom based multinational. Acquired with the Bookers take-over were lands and mills accounting for some 85% of the nation's sugar production, the leading retail stores group, as well as enterprises in distilling, drug manufacturing, shrimping, dairy products, cattle ranching, printing, shipping, insurance and other fields. At this point the only remaining foreign holdings of any magnitude were in the banking and insurance fields. Some three quarters of the nation's production of goods and services was now in government hands.[49] All nationalization had been carried out through compensation agreements with the companies concerned, with payments spread over a period of time.

Guyana's shift away from assumptions of continued reliance on close economic and political linkage with developed western nations was signaled not only by the nationalizations, but also by active participation in the nonaligned movement. Prime Minister Burnham led a Guyanese delegation to the Lusaka Conference of Non-Aligned Nations, held in September 1970, with Guyana the only western hemisphere nation fully participating in the conference with its political leader in attendance. Guyana had been a member of the sixteen-nation standing committee preparing for the meeting.

Georgetown itself became a center for nonaligned activity when in August 1972 Guyana hosted the Conference of Foreign Ministers of Non-Aligned Countries, a conference resulting in "The Georgetown Declaration, the Action Programme for Economic Co-operation."[50] Guyana's continued active involvement in the nonaligned movement was signified by her designation, at a meeting of the Standing Committee of Non-Aligned countries in December 1972, as responsible for follow-up and implementation of trade, industry, and transport aspects of the Action Programme,[51] and by her active participation in the Algiers (1973) and Sri Lanka (1976) Conferences of Non-Aligned Nations.

At the general election held July 16, 1973 (within the five-year period since the 1968 election mandated by the constitution), Burnham's People's National Congress Party claimed a sweeping victory. According to the announced results, the PNC was allotted thirty-seven of the fifty-three seats in the National Assembly, giving it the two-thirds margin required for certain types of constitutional amendment, which it had sought. The PPP was allocated fourteen seats and the Guyana Liberator Party, a new group into which the United Force had been amalgamated, two seats. Another new party, formed by former PNC activist and Home Affairs Minister Llewellyn John, the People's Democratic Movement, received no seat.[52]

There is probably no more reason to take the results of the 1973 election at face value than in the case of the 1968 vote. The weekly political and economic report from London, *Latin America*, asserted:

> There now seems to be clear evidence, not only from the three opposition parties, but also from independent foreign observers and even from some backers of the government, that prime minister Forbes Burnham only won a two thirds majority in the general election on 16 July through widespread fraud in the voting.
>
> It was a repeat of the 1968 poll: ballot boxes were broken open by supporters of Burnham's People's National Congress (PNC) party and packed with bundles of votes for the government; postal voting lists were not available for inspection until the day before the election; the government refused the opposition's demand that the votes be counted on the spot at the polling stations to prevent

fraud; thousands of people discovered that their ballots had already been cast by unauthorized proxies while others, overwhelmingly opposition supporters, were simply turned away at the polling stations; and samples suggested that nearly half the 33,000 people listed as overseas voters did not exist. In Britain, even Jamaicans were added to the roll. Not surprisingly, the government claimed it won a breathtaking 98 percent of the overseas vote, which is nearly one tenth of the total electorate and, under the proportional representation system, worth four seats in parliament.[53]

Commenting on the elections, *Keesing's Contemporary Archives* stated:

> Misconduct in the elections was also alleged by British observers in particular in connexion with the registration of 33,000 Guyanese voters overseas (18,000 of them in Britain)—out of a total electorate of 420,000—who under the proportional representation system accounted for four seats. The Guyana High Commission in London subsequently denied that the registration list of voters in Britain had contained the errors alleged. Mr. Burnham had on July 15 revoked an earlier undertaking to have the votes counted at each of the 381 polling stations and had ordered all ballot boxes to be taken to counting centres in Georgetown.[54]

Two men were shot and killed on Election Day, reportedly when they tried to prevent authorities from taking ballot boxes from polling stations.[55]

A "white paper" on the 1973 election was published by the People's Progressive Party in October of that year, alleging faulty and fraudulent election procedures, especially those involving security of ballot boxes between the end of voting and the counting many hours later.[56] The white paper quotes Ric Mentus, then editor of the *Sunday Graphic,* writing in that publication's issue of July 22, 1973, as follows:

> In an election that was remarkable for the spate of controversy it generated from the initial stages of registration of voters right through to the final counting of ballots, both the nature and scope of the irregularities reported are serious enough to demand an impartial inquiry into the entire electoral process. . . the whole nation is perplexed over the double standards being applied to the elections procedure and results. The people cannot stretch credibility far enough to embrace both the details of irregularities that they have experienced and the 'persistent suggestion and indoctrination' that has been coming from all official and semi-official circles. The mind boggles at the enormity of the task and the Guyanese after the election is sadder and a bit more fearful of the future.[57]

Critical commentary on the election by Rickey Singh, probably then Guyana's most widely respected journalist, also appeared in the *Sunday Graphic* of July 22. (Singh was, as of the end of 1973, transferred to Trinidad by the Thompson Newspaper Group, owners of the *Graphic*, to work on the Group's *Trinidad Guardian*). Singh concluded his article:

> Why bother with any attempt to analyse the election. . . . The question is: From here where? The shame is greater than the victory, said one leading Guyanese writer.[58]

In his last report for the *Graphic* (December 30, 1973), Singh, after asserting that "the [1973] election really proved nothing significantly new," stated:

> What I mean is that the racial divisions that existed prior to July 16, are still there. In spite of the plethora of platitudes, the manoeuverings and the headlines, our major ethnic communities are still as polarised as ever.
>
> The *de facto* one-party state in an allegedly multi-party system of government has not changed. In fact, if anything, the election in July served the undesirable (or desirable, according to your point of view) purpose of giving that *de facto* situation a *de jure* status.[59]

The three opposition parties issued a statement rejecting the announced results of the election and declaring that the two parties which had been allocated seats would not take them up. However, the leader of the United Force Party, Mr. Feilden Singh, and UF member Eleanor DaSilva later assumed the two Liberator Party seats in Parliament, constituting the only seated opposition until May 1976, when the People's Progressive Party ended its parliamentary boycott.

Following the election, with the PNC holding the necessary two-thirds majority in the National Assembly, the constitution was amended by reducing the voting age from twenty-one to eighteen and by abolishing appeals to Great Britain's Privy Council from judgments of Guyanese courts. Prior to the election the PPP had blocked the age-reduction amendment, fearing the PNC would gain an advantage by controlling registration of the youth. Likewise, it had opposed abolition of Privy Council appeals on the ground that under current circumstances the appeal provided a necessary safeguard in Guyana's judicial system.

A major innovation in national life, a system of national service, the first such program in the Commonwealth Caribbean, was put forward in a State Paper in December 1973. Getting underway in the Fall of 1974, the plan, while initially voluntary, entails compulsory service of youths in a variety of training and work programs. Emphasis in the program is upon involvement in national development (including obtaining needed skills), especially in regard to opening up and bringing into production new agricultural settlements in the nation's hinterland (interior).[60]

The world economic crisis, which had been intensified by oil price hikes in the Fall of 1973, with especially adverse impact on non-oil-producing developing countries, necessitated the imposition of import restrictions in addition to those already in effect and a tightening of currency controls. In announcing the restrictions in January 1974, Prime Minister Burnham stressed the seriousness of the threat to the nation's economy, stating: "The situation today is very much akin to war. We must, if we are to survive, accept the restrictions and sacrifices of a war-time economy."[61] Dr. Kenneth King, Guyana's minister of economic development, repeating the appeal for sacrifices three days later, stated that total expenditures required to achieve targets set in the country's second development plan (for the period 1972-76) would have to be increased from $1.1 billion Guyanese (equivalent to one-half this amount in U.S. dollars) to $1.7 billion Guyanese, with $100 million of this increase needed during 1974.[62]

Various factors, including an upturn in sugar prices and increases in production in various sectors, resulted in a doubling of the value of exports of goods for 1974, with net holdings of international reserves increasing $63.6 million (Guyanese) that year, as contrasted with a decrease of $47.9 million for 1973.[63] For 1975 the trends were again favorable, although a Bank of Guyana report noted that the recovery from the depressed output levels of 1973, begun in 1974, continued "at a considerably reduced rate."[64] Net international reserves stood at $197.7 million as of year-end 1975, up $92.3 million from the previous year.[65] However, 1976 was characterized in the year-end budget speech of the Minister of Finance as "a bad year for production," and a drop in international reserves of some $250 million was foreseen.[66]

In one of the most dramatic developments of Guyana's recent history, Cheddi Jagan announced in August 1975 a shift on the part of his People's Progressive Party from outright opposition to the Burnham-PNC government to "critical support." He and Prime Minister Burnham appeared on the same platform at the May 26, 1976 independence anniversary observations, with huge portraits of both leaders overhead. The dominant theme of slogans posted prominently and of speeches of the period was the need to combat imperialism and "destabilization" efforts orchestrated from abroad. The PPP had taken up its seats in parliament two days earlier, with Jagan slated to resume his position as Leader of the Opposition.

Thus, the first post-independence decade ended with the two figures who have dominated Guyanese politics for over a quarter of a century once again in a form of partnership and with their respective political parties in a posture of détente. However, as in the case of many other new nations (and not a few of the older ones), a multitude of problems awaited resolution, whether by efforts of the old generation of leadership or by the work of new and as yet largely untested hands.

Chapter 2

Political Leadership for the New Nation

Throughout the post-independence decade the only political parties represented in Parliament have been the People's National Congress (PNC), the People's Progressive Party (PPP), and the United Force (UF). In 1975, toward the end of the period, a new political movement highly critical of government policy, the Working People's Alliance, was formed. Forbes Burnham and Cheddi Jagan have been the dominant figures in their parties during the full ten years. Fielden Singh has had United Force leadership since the mid-1969 resignation of party founder (and Guyana's leading businessman) Peter d'Aguiar. The best known figure of the Working People's Alliance, Eusi Kwayana, has been active in Guyanese politics since as early as 1947.

Linden Forbes Sampson Burnham is an impressive political figure by any standard. He has insight, intelligence, and a drive for power that would be hard to match. Combined with these qualities is an oratorical style which has been described even by critics as among the best in the English-speaking world.[1] Born in 1923 in Kitty, an Atlantic coast village and suburb of Georgetown, his father was headmaster of the local Methodist primary school. He attended Queen's College, Guyana's top boys school, from 1935 to 1942, in which year he won the honor accorded only one person per year in the country, the Guiana Scholarship. The coveted award provided for university education in England. (It is interesting to note that some ten years earlier, Eric Williams, Trinidad's scholar-prime minister, had won the same award in that country.) An introduction to Burnham's collected speeches, *A Destiny to Mould*, points out that "Like some 31 per cent of Guyana's population of three-quarters of a million, he is a direct descent of one of the thousands of African slaves brought by the Dutch and British to work the sugar plantations of the South American colony."[2]

In view of wartime circumstances, Burnham did not commence studies in England immediately, instead joining the teaching staff at Queens College and pursuing a London University bachelors degree on an external basis. He received the B.A. in 1944 and in 1945 traveled to England to take up studies in law at the University of London. As a student at Queen's College, Burnham had been president of the Literary and Debating Society as well as editor of the College magazine. He continued his oratorical activities in London, winning the best speaker's cup of the Laws Faculty. He was also active in student affairs, becoming president of the West Indian Student Union and a delegate to the International Union of Students' Congresses in Prague (1947) and Paris (1948).[3] He received the LL.B. degree with honors in 1947 and in 1948, associated with Gray's Inn, was called to the bar.

Returning to Guyana in 1949, Burnham set up a law practice and plunged into political activities. He joined forces that same year with Cheddi Jagan, and they transformed the Political Affairs Committee in which Jagan was a dominant force into the People's Progressive Party, with Jagan as leader and Burnham as chairman. The split of this party into two factions, one led by Jagan and the other by Burnham, in 1955, and the subsequent name change, in 1957, of Burnham's group to the People's National Congress, as well as electoral developments since that time, have been discussed in the introductory chapter.

Burnham also became active in labor union affairs, serving as president of the Guyana Labour Union from 1952 to 1956 and from 1963 to 1965. He continues as president on leave. From 1959 to 1964 he was Mayor of Georgetown, the youngest person to hold that post to that point, and in 1959 served as president of the British Guiana Bar Association. In 1960, he "took silk," being decreed a Queen's Counsel. He was Leader of the Opposition in the 1957-61 and 1961-64 legislatures. Burnham has been married twice. His first marriage, in 1951, resulted in three daughters and ended in divorce. Married again in 1967, he has since become father to two more daughters. He lists his religion as Methodist.[4]

Dr. Cheddi Jagan possesses charisma in ample measure and a personal charm and warmth that constitute undeniable political assets. His dedication to social change in Guyana is of such long standing that few in that country deny him a place of honor among Guyana's modern political heroes. Yet, he seems to have lacked not only the backing of the near-at-hand and powerful United States, an essential ingredient to Burnham's assumption of power and, at least for the first few years, continuation in power, but also qualities of political acumen Burnham has evidenced in substantial measure.[5]

Born in 1918 of East Indian parents at Port Mourant, in the heart of the sugar lands of the county of Berbice, Jagan has written, in his political biography, *The West on Trial*,[6] of the experiences of his father and mother as workers in the cane fields.[7] Both of his grandmothers had arrived from India as indentured immigrants in 1901, and they too had worked in the fields. Eventually Jagan's father became a "driver," placing him, according to Jagan, at the "lowest level of the middle stratum" of a cane cutting gang.[8] Jagan states that both his parents were Hindus and deeply religious. They had been married when his father was ten and his mother slightly younger, following the tradition of the time, but did not live together until his mother was about sixteen.[9]

Jagan first went to an Anglican primary school in Port Mourant, then to Scots School in nearby Rose Hall, then to a private secondary school in Port Mourant, and finally, at the age of fifteen, was sent to Queen's College, about a hundred miles from home, in Georgetown. At Port Mourant, Jagan reports that poverty had been intense—he had not worn shoes until the age of twelve—but in Georgetown he began to develop a kind of snobbery and to partake of the values of Queen's College and the families with whom he boarded.[10]

Completing his studies at Queen's in 1935, Jagan the following year set out for the United States and a two-year pre-dental course at Howard University. His father provided $500 for passage and for expenses while studying, and Jagan won a free tuition scholarship for his second year at Howard. Thereafter, he entered Northwestern University Dental School. While at Northwestern he also studied social sciences at the Y.M.C.A. College. In 1943 he married Janet Rosenberg, then a proofreader at the American Medical Association offices. He notes that "We did not have the consent of parents on either side. Janet's father had threatened to shoot me. My parents too, were unhappy."[11] The new dentist returned home in October 1943 and was able to send passage money in time for his wife to join him just before Christmas. With antiquated equipment acquired before departing from the United States, he set up his practice in Georgetown, a practice that he has continued as time permitted throughout his political career.

Jagan traces his ideological development in *The West on Trial*, referring to experiences with racism in the United States, especially when in the company of black friends, and to observations of poverty for both blacks and whites. In his readings during the Y.M.C.A. College days, he refers to the influence of Charles Beard's works, Nehru's autobiography, *Toward Freedom*, Matthew Josephson's *Robber Barons*, and George Seldes' weekly *In Fact*. He comments that *"In Fact* had given me a new perspective of America and of the world, and a peep into socialism. Karl Marx's *Capital* was later to open up whole new horizons."[12]

Back in Georgetown, the Jagans found the closing years of the war a time of intellectual ferment. They began to attract attention through participation in the Carnegie Library weekly discussion circle and through letters to the press. Janet Jagan's espousal of birth control brought heavy criticism from Catholic quarters, which Dr. Jagan asserts was expressed in anticommunist terms.[13]

In 1946 Dr. Jagan and others formed the Political Affairs Committee, the name being adopted from the Political Action Committee of the Congress of Industrial Organizations in the United States.[14] He fought for a seat in the newly constituted Legislative Council in 1947, narrowly defeating his opponent John d'Aguiar, a leading figure in local business, and served in the Council until 1953, when national elections were again held.

The linkup between the Jagans and Burnham, after the latter's return to Guyana in 1949, first within the Political Affairs Committee, then from 1950 to 1955 within the People's Progressive Party, has been mentioned previously. Following the suspension of the constitution in October 1953, Jagan and Burnham traveled to England, attending the House of Commons debate on suspension, and from there went on to India, where their visit involved a tour of the major cities and addressing an informal session of both houses of Parliament, with Prime Minister Nehru in the chair.[15] Several People's Progressive Party leaders were jailed in the aftermath of the constitution's suspension, and eventually, in 1954, Jagan himself spent five months in jail for violating an order restricting his movements to Georgetown.[16]

His party having received the majority of seats in the Legislative Council in the 1957 election, Jagan served from that point until the 1961 election as Minister of Trade and Industry and toward the end of this period had the title of Chief Minister. Under a revised governmental organization after the 1961 election, in which the PPP again prevailed, he was Premier, remaining in that office until loss of power to the PNC-UF coalition in late 1964. He served as leader of the parliamentary opposition until after the 1973 election when his party refused to take seats in the National Assembly. Following the PPP's return to the Assembly in May 1976, he resumed the opposition leadership.

Like Burnham, Jagan has been active in labor union affairs. For a period in 1945 he served as treasurer of the Manpower Citizens Association, representing sugar workers, and in 1949 he became president of the Sawmill Workers' Union, later called the Sawmill and Forest Workers' union.[17]

Janet Jagan has remained active in Guyanese and People's Progressive Party politics, serving as Deputy Speaker of the House of Assembly in 1953, Minister of Labour, Health and Housing from 1957-61, and in 1963-64 as Minister of Home Affairs.[18] She has been editor of the party daily newspaper, *Mirror*. With the PPP's return to parliament in 1976 she took up a National Assembly seat. At that time she was secretary for international affairs of the PPP. The Jagans have one son and one daughter. The son, Cheddi Jr., better known as Joe, figured prominently in an incident at Sir George Williams University, Montreal, which became an impelling factor in the development of the black power movement in the Commonwealth Caribbean, to be further discussed in a later chapter.

Feilden Singh, United Force leader, succeeded to that post after the resignation of the party's founder and Guyana's leading businessman, Peter d'Aguiar, in mid-1969. During the PPP's parliamentary absence, he served as Leader of the opposition in the National Assembly from the Spring of 1974 to May 1976. East Indian ethnically, he is, as is d'Aguiar, Roman Catholic. His brother Benedit Singh became, in 1971, the first Catholic bishop of Guyanese background.

A practicing barrister, Singh was born in 1932 in Buxton, on the Atlantic coast about fifteen miles east of Georgetown. He received his high school education at St. Stanislaus College, a Catholic school in Georgetown. After working for three years as an accounts clerk with the Rice Marketing Board and for several more years on the bureaucracy of the country's court system, he went to England to study law, being admitted to the bar through Lincoln's Inn in 1962. He was a United Force candidate for a seat in the legislature in the 1964 election but did not get one of the seven seats which the party won. However, in 1966 he gained a seat on the resignation of a UF member. In 1965 he had served as legal advisor to the United Force delegation to the independence conference in London, and after taking a seat in the National Assembly served as Minister of Works and Hydraulics in the coalition government. Following the 1968 election he held one of the four seats accorded the United Force and after the 1973 election took one of the two seats allotted to the Liberator Party, with which the UF had merged for election purposes.[19]

Eusi Kwayana, a leading figure of the Working People's Alliance (WPA) since its formation in 1975, is a schoolteacher by profession. He was active in the People's Progressive Party, serving as assistant general secretary in 1953. Splitting with Jagan and the PPP in 1957, he ran as an independent in elections held that year but failed to win a seat. For several years thereafter he was active in Burnham's People's National Congress party, becoming general secretary. However, he withdrew as a candidate for the PNC in the 1961 election and was expelled from the party. After Jagan's victory in the 1961 election, he and others formed the Society for Racial Equality, a group which, apparently fearing East Indian domination of the country, proposed partition into African, East Indian and "free" zones.

In 1964 Kwayana formed the Association for Social and Cultural Relations with Independent Africa (ASCRIA), an organization he has headed since that time. Apparently he had an important role in support of the PNC's election performance in 1964. Thereafter, he accepted appointments as chairman of a land distribution committee and of the Guyana Marketing Corporation. However, complaining of corruption in high places, he eventually, in April 1973, split with the PNC government. Guyanese political scientist J.E. Greene refers to Kwayana as a person of "great leadership legitimacy in view of his universal reputation for incorruptible honesty."[20]

The Organization of the Working People's Alliance brought into association Kwayana's ASCRIA, the Ratoon group of scholars, in which Clive

Thomas, University of Guyana economist, and Walter Rodney, a historian of far-ranging reputation, are best known, the Indian Political Revolutionary Associates, headed by Moses Bhagwan, and the Working People's Vanguard Party (ML), led by Brindley Benn. The WPA has published, against considerable government resistance (in the form of searches, seizures and court actions) a newspaper known as *Dayclean*.[21]

The paper has ceaselessly attacked the PNC government, accusing it of acting contrary to the interests of the nation's working people, among other things, in not nationalizing Bookers sugar holdings earlier than it did, in "buying out" with excessive compensation firms nationalized, in pursuing policies that have led to low wages and high costs of living, and in repressing movements of the landless to obtain holdings.[22]

Cheddi Jagan and the PPP have always maintained a strong socialist image, but until 1969, there was some controversy, both within and outside Guyana, over whether the party should be regarded as Marxist in an eclectic and reformist sense or Marxist-Leninist, with or without a Moscow affiliation. Since June of that year, however, when Jagan headed a two-man PPP delegation to the long postponed and much heralded World Conference of Communist and Workers Parties in Moscow and signed the Conference's final declaration, "The Tasks of the Struggle against Imperialism at the Present Stage, and the Unity of Action of the Communist and Workers' Parties and of all Anti-Imperialist Forces," there has been no doubt either as to the party's Marxist-Leninism or as to its Moscow affiliation.

Speaking at the Moscow conference, Jagan declared:

> For us, this is like homecoming, like joining our ideological family.
>
> Not only theory, but practice also, has taught us that this is where we belong. Repeated attacks against us by the conservative Churchill, MacMillan and Hume governments, and by the liberal Kennedy administration, and betrayal by the social democratic Attlee and Wilson governments have established that only the international communist movement in alliance with the democratic and progressive forces in the capitalist states, and the liberation movements in the colonial and neocolonial countries, and not conservative, liberal or social-democratic leadership can liberate the working people of Guyana and elsewhere from imperialist exploitation and oppression.[23]

Later in 1969, Jagan writing in the PPP's quarterly journal, *Thunder*, advised that "It is imperative that national liberation parties in other third-world countries like Guyana follow the lead of PPP, begin to transform themselves from loose, mass parties into vanguard Marxist-Leninist type of parties and develop the closest links with the socialist system."[24]

The United Force Party has generally been considered the most conservative of the political forces in Guyana, supporting a capitalist economy.[25] The People's National Congress party, on the other hand, for some years took a course between that of the UF and the PPP. A 1960 pamphlet declared "we in the People's National Congress refuse to be doctrinaire, we refuse to join hands with those who believe that the state must own all the means of production or to join hands with those who contend that private enterprise must be allowed to run amok...."[26] The "neither-nor" course was still evident when, in August 1969, Burnham declared at a regional PNC meeting:

> Our ideology, our economic and political goal can be described as socialist because of what we seek to establish. Since, however, we have a different social and economic structure, qualitatively from that obtaining in European countries, we cannot and must not put ourselves into the strait jackets of their dogmas and tactics. We will, as a result, be suspect by both sides, who would like to continue a form of intellectual, if not also economic, colonialism, but that suspicion is the price we must pay if we are to fashion our own destinies and work out our own solutions. It is easy to shout, for international consumption, that we are capitalist, Marxist, socialist or communist and attract international notice. But of what concrete value are international plaudits to us?
>
> In moving towards our goal of exploiting our resources and giving the masses economic power, we shall have to fashion new institutions, re-fashion old ones and put new content into others which already exist. The cooperative is one of the latter. It has to be expanded and adapted and given a new purpose. Investment by coops need not and must not be limited to agriculture and consumer goods but should extend into industry of all types. From the right and left there will be criticisms and caveats which are in fact rationalised prejudices. But we must know where we are going and see to it that we use our own vehicle to get there. Your government is committed irrevocably to widening and strengthening the cooperative sector.[27]

The PNC, in a new constitution approved in December 1974, declared itself to be a socialist party. Socialism was defined primarily in terms of commitments to securing and maintaining "through the practice of cooperative socialism," the interests, well-being and prosperity of the people of Guyana and to assuring that the people of the nation "own and control for their benefit" its natural resources.[28] At the same party congress at which the constitution was approved, Burnham stressed the distinction between capitalism and socialism as being that "the former contemplates, and is primarily based on, the production of goods and services for profit to the individual, while the latter premises production for the use and service to people, to human beings."[29] Stressing that since the PNC was a socialist party "its members, and more particularly its leaders, cannot be involved in ruthless private profit hunting," he outlined a code regulating the conduct of party members and leaders.[30]

At the PNC's first biennial congress, held in August 1975, Burnham made clear his view that while the PNC was committed to achieving socialism in Guyana, the transition would take time, pointing out that in some countries this had required twenty to twenty-five years, in others ten to fifteen. However, he asserted that "the atmosphere and circumstances appear to be conducive to our moving to socialism in a shorter time than many who have gone that route before us," stating, after referring to other favorable factors, that "it is apposite to note that in the last five years at least, the camp of Socialism has been considerably strengthened throughout the world."[31]

Earlier the same month, Cheddi Jagan, speaking as party secretary general at the PPP's twenty-fifth anniversary conference, while expressing a variety of criticisms regarding PNC policies and their execution, declared that various changes, among them the nationalization of Reynolds bauxite holdings, required a reassessment of his party's stance. He declared that:

> The situation now therefore demands a more flexible approach on the part of the PPP. The party had previously declared that it does not have a monopoly on socialism, that it is prepared regardless of ideological and tactical differences to work with others if they are interested in building a socialist Guyana. And this included the PNC.
>
> Our political line should be changed from non-cooperation and civil resistance to critical support. This can lay the basis for a political solution in our country. It will also help to frustrate the PNC's attempts to isolate the Party.
>
> If we continue with the old line we face the danger in the new situation of opposing for the sake of opposing and thus playing into the hands of the reactionaries. As revolutionaries, we cannot oppose any and every move just because we are opposed to the PNC.[32]

Reflecting on developments less than a year later at the tenth anniversary of independence, with nationalization of Bookers holdings complete and with the PPP's critical support continuing in effect, Burnham may well have harbored the conviction that for Guyana the pace of transition to socialism was indeed quickening.

Chapter 3

Enhancing Regional Ties

"The commitment to Caribbean unity is one of the main features of Guyanese foreign policy."[1] Thus opened the first section of the first issue of *Guyana Journal*, published by Guyana's Ministry of External Affairs in April 1968. The *Journal* item probably would have been more accurate if it had asserted that a commitment to Caribbean (meaning specifically Commonwealth Caribbean) unity was the *prime* element of Guyanese foreign policy at that time, such was the dedication of Forbes Burnham and the government he led to this goal. Within a few years, active participation in the nonaligned movement would challenge and perhaps displace the priority given pursuit of regional unity, although the two enterprises are not necessarily incompatible and the nonaligned thrust can in many ways be regarded as a logical extension of Guyana's regional policies.

As noted in the introductory chapter, Guyana was not a member of the West Indies federation during the federation's brief life-span, 1958-62.[2] However, Burnham, who had unsuccessfully championed in the British Guiana Legislative Council in 1958 his country's involvement in the federation, had no sooner become premier, following the election of late 1964, than he undertook an initiative for Commonwealth Caribbean integration. Discussions with Barbados' premier Errol Barrow led to an agreement involving Barbados, Antigua, and Guyana, signed in December 1965, for establishment of a free trade area known as CARIFTA, the Caribbean Free Trade Area. The agreement was intended to be open-ended in terms of further membership, at least for the Commonwealth Caribbean. After Guyana and Barbados attained independence in 1966, the three-party CARIFTA pact, unimplemented and largely symbolic, took on life when, with substantial revamping, a new agreement came into effect May 1, 1968, and Trinidad and Tobago joined the group. Dominica, Grenada, St. Kitts-Nevis, St. Lucia and St. Vincent followed on July 1, all of them then associated states, a status acquired in early 1967 providing for internal autonomy, with Britain continuing with defense and foreign affairs responsibilities. (Grenada became independent in February

1974.) Jamaica, like Trinidad and Tobago independent since 1962, and Monserrat, at the time still a colony of Britain, joined on August 1, 1968, and Belize (formerly known as British Honduras) in May 1971. Headquarters for the Commonwealth Caribbean Regional Secretariat, coordinating CARIFTA and other Commonwealth Caribbean activities, were established in Georgetown in March 1969.

CARIFTA was transformed, effective August 1, 1973, into CARICOM, the Caribbean Community, involving not only a free trade area but establishment of a common external tariff as well as coordination of location of new industry in the region and of trade and foreign policies. Georgetown continued as the center of Commonwealth Caribbean regional activities, with the Commonwealth Caribbean Regional Secretariat renamed the Caribbean Community Secretariat. Parallel with CARIFTA and CARICOM developments, and closely related to them, the Caribbean Development Bank was established in 1979 with headquarters in Barbados.[3]

For a time, at least, Prime Minister Burnham's interest in regional integration was by no means limited to economic matters, or to mere cooperation and coordination of policies among members. He was explicit in asserting the necessity of political integration as well. Speaking in the March 1967 National Assembly debate on foreign policy, Burnham said:

> I have recently come from the Caribbean and I have had the opportunity of assessing at first-hand the response not only of Caribbean governments but of Caribbean people (a) to Guyana's participation with the rest of the Caribbean in exercises like this and (b) to the concept of a Caribbean nation. In these days when already independent, large and, in some cases, powerful nations are seeking to come together, it seems elementary that such an exercise is desirable in the Caribbean.
>
> It is true that the federation came to grief but it is also true that the West Indian people in fields other than cricket or in addition to the field of cricket, are most anxious that there be a coming together. We do not underestimate the difficulties. We do not for one moment attempt to ignore the individual problems which may arise, but of this we are sure, that the fact of a Caribbean nation will be in our time. And, secondly, that Guyana is in a peculiar position to make a tremendous and significant contribution to the achievement of that fact.[4]

Burnham reiterated his belief in the urgency of political unity when, in speaking to the annual meeting of the People's National Congress in April 1971, he stated:

> I may be considered a visionary, but economic integration in my judgement must lead to political integration or unity.
>
> The old West Indian Federation broke up for a number of different or complementary reasons among which was the fact that its form resulted more from a British imposition than a West Indian consensus. Now, however, the urgency of the West Indian and world situations dictates unity. The form this unity takes in political and constitutional terms need not be that of the 1958-62 Federation, nor again some half-baked copy of the Australian, Canadian and American models. It must fit our needs in the Region.
>
> On Sunday, 10th April, 1966, on the eve of Independence at the tenth Annual Congress of the PNC, I said that this Party was prepared to agree to a limitation of Guyana's sovereignty in the interest of political unity in the Caribbean. That still remains our position and our interest is still in contributing, not in leading.[5]

An ill-fated attempt at political unification was made in 1971. With Guyana leading the way, her Attorney General and Minister of State S.S. Ramphal having drafted the agreement, and with most of the Eastern Caribbean islands having associated state status as parties, the "Grenada Declaration" was signed on July 25th.[6] The declaration was intended to set in motion a process under which the subscribing entities and such other Commonwealth Caribbean polities as joined would form a new West Indian nation. However, with Guyana the only independent nation in the subscribing group, and with defections from the original subscribers, the project collapsed.[7]

Cheddi Jagan's position on regional integration has not paralleled Burnham's. While he has indicated support for integration, even federation, in principle, he has found the circumstances and types of integration proposed in the 1940's, 1950's, 1960's, and now the 1970's not to his liking.

Speaking in the Legislative Council in 1948, in regard to British Guiana's involvement in a West Indies federation, then being considered, he stated:

> ... I am not in agreement with the proposed federation—closer union or closer association—as enunciated by the vested interests. That would merely mean the pooling of a few services and leaving the Colonies to be the swimming pool of outside capital. My view of federation is that we should have a strong federal body which would have certain powers delegated to it by several units—a strong federal body having that power with Dominion status, and with each of the units having internal self government. That is the federation with which I am in agreement.[8]

Ten years later, in 1958, Jagan spoke in the Legislative Council in opposition to a resolution put forward by Burnham under which the British Guiana government would be urged to enter into negotiations with a view to immediate admission to the West Indies Federation. Jagan stated:

> The P.P.P. says that Federation under Crown Colony Government can never succeed. We say: let us have Dominion status before we start talking about Federation, and let us have internal self-government in order to remove the shackles first. If the West Indian leaders demanded Dominion status now they would get it, not because the British Government is so generous but because of the trend of things. . . .
>
> It is high time in this country and in the West Indies all political leaders join themselves together and demand independence now, as then, so far as British Guiana and the People's Progressive Party are concerned, the Federation would become a reality.[9]

When the 1965 agreement providing for the mini-CARIFTA of Antigua, Barbados, and Guyana came before the National Assembly in December 1966, the PPP, rather than opposing this step toward integration, abstained. Among the reasons Jagan gave for the PPP's inability to support affirmatively the pact were the small scale of integration involved and the asserted disadvantage to Guyanese manufacturers in relation to large corporations (Unilever was mentioned as an example) operating under the free trade zone umbrella.[10] Commenting on the mixed emotions with which his party viewed the agreement, Jagan said:

> We would like to make our position very clear. We say that unity is necessary, but not unity at any price. There are all kinds of unity. We have an example of unity on the Government benches [referring to the PNC-UF coalition], and we see where this unity is leading this country today. As we see it, this unity which is limited to three relatively small territories will hardly achieve anything, and the unity which is projected is unity at the trade level more or less in a vacuum without interfering with the social economic structure of these countries, so we have very mixed feelings on this whole question.
>
> While we agree that unity is essential if progress is to be made, we realise that that unity must be a qualitative type of unity where other structural changes will take place. What is projected here is a unity which we see will not lead to any progress or any forward movement. Indeed, it can be a retrogressive move, and can lead to further binding of the chains of the people of these territories.[11]

In a seventy-two page commentary on the "Grenada Declaration" and related Caribbean integration developments published in February 1972, Jagan declared:

> The formation of CARIFTA was in keeping with the new strategy of US imperialism—the creation of Common Markets and Free Trade Areas to benefit its multinational corporations and to rationalize and stabilize world capitalism and imperialism as a socio-economic system. It is not to be forgotten that L.F.S. Burnham, the chief protagonist of CARIFTA, had been brought to power in Guyana with the help of US imperialism and was committed to pro-imperialist domestic and foreign policies.[12]

Continuing his critique, Jagan asserted:

> CARIFTA has admittedly failed. Rather, it has succeeded within the narrow limits set by imperialism—the branch plants of the foreign companies, established in Jamaica and Trinidad and to a lesser degree in Barbados, have prospered with the elimination of tarriff walls.
>
> At the end of the first two years, Jamaica increased her exports by nearly 60 per cent, Trinidad by over 30 per cent and Guyana by a mere 5 per cent. . . .
>
> Guyana. . . has been caught in an imperialist squeeze. Despite the demagogy of the Burnham regime about socialism, people's ownership and control of natural resources, "cooperative republic," and self reliance, Guyana, like Belize, under the imperialist plan for the Caribbean has been relegated to the role of an agricultural producer to an industrialized West Indies.[13]

The United Force party, as part of the coalition government, had voted for approval of the CARIFTA agreement by the National Assembly in December 1966 and has apparently continued to support integration efforts since the coalition's termination in late 1968.

Guyana's benefits from the regional integration were clearly not of an economic nature, at least during the early years. Noting the failure of exports from Guyana to regional partners to grow in any appreciable extent in the 1967-70 period, in contrast to regional export gains by Jamaica, Trinidad and Tobago, and Barbados, a report by the regional secretariat stated that

> Guyana was at the beginning of CARIFTA less advanced in the manufacturing sector, particularly in those products that could be readily exported to CARIFTA, than Jamaica, Trinidad and Tobago

and Barbados. Here we should note that Guyana's ability to sell significant quantities of products to the CARIFTA markets is likely to manifest itself over the long run, as its agricultural sector and resource-based industries develop. These sectors and industries are now in the process of development. Examples are animal feeding stuffs, timber and timber-based industries, iron ore, leather, glass, etc. Generalising from the case of Guyana, we may say that the full regional potential can be developed only on a long-term basis and within the framework of regional policies that make for planned complementarity of the economies of the member countries.[14]

Prime Minister Burnham had in fact opted for long-term benefits when, in addressing the annual conference of his party in April 1971, he stated:

> We in the PNC are prepared to make sacrifices in the cause of greater regional good. Guyana reaps little or no immediate material benefit from CARIFTA, but we look to the day when all West Indians will reap benefits from a flourishing integrated economy.[15]

In terms of indirect gains, the role of the Commonwealth Community Secretariat (prior to CARICOM, known as the Commonwealth Caribbean Secretariat) is worthy of special attention. Guyana has capable economists and planners, but these are in short supply in any developing nation. Thus, the location in Georgetown of the Secretariat, with such outstanding economists as William Demas and Alistair McIntyre serving as secretary-general, has doubtless been an important, and (from Burnham's viewpoint) hardly unintended, benefit. A former official of the secretariat advised me that Burnham and his government were not hesitant to seek assistance from the secretariat on national matters, with the line between secretariat service and Guyana government service sometimes blurred, at least in the government's eyes. On the other hand, the Guyana government, according to Demas, has shown a willingness to release key personnel to assist the secretariat, "a willingness not always matched by other regional governments."[16]

In terms of national identity, the regional integration movement may have assisted in further development of a sense of West Indianness already characteristic, especially among the intellectuals of the area, and thus may have contributed to overcoming the ever-present danger of re-intensification of ethnic conflict in Guyana. Commenting before any impact from CARIFTA was likely, Aaron Segal had noted in 1968 that

> among West Indian intellectuals there is a growing sense of regional self-consciousness. As ties with England diminish these intellectuals are increasingly concerned with a psychological and emotional

search for identity. It is inadequate to be "Guyanese", "Trinidadian" or "Jamaican," particularly when in Canada, England and the United States the experience of migration, racial discrimination, and contact with other West Indians has contributed to a new sense of identity. There is more status and solidarity in a dual national and regional identity, a wistful desire to "feel at home anywhere in the West Indies." Hugh Springer, former registrar of UWI [University of the West Indies], asserts that "our common origins and associations have created and are in process of molding a people. This is shown in our way of life, our food and drink, our sport, our recreations, our arts. Our poets, novelists, playwrights, dancers, painters, and sculptors are recognizably West Indian." The rising generation of post-independence intellectuals, increasingly receiving their initial university education at UWI, is concerned that it is not enough to have a national identity. They are highly aware of the constraints of small size, particularly in relation to modern technology.[17]

Whether the current level of integration under CARICOM has converted ethnic (or national) identity within Guyana into regional identity to any substantial degree is questionable. However, the attention focused on CARIFTA and CARICOM has doubtless had some impact in diverting attention from narrow ethnic concerns. Further, the region's capability of providing a spatial dimension conducive to relieving ethnic and, perhaps, ideological tensions should be recognized. In their study of prospects for regional integration, West Indian economists Havelock Brewster and Clive Thomas, the latter from Guyana, have noted that "One painful inheritance of slavery is the claustrophobia of size and our response to it; size not in the sense of measurable phenomena but in the sense of the degrees of psychological freedom which a man has without endangering his creative survival."[18]

Possible linkage between Burnham's aggressive pursuit of regional integration and control of Guyana's territory had been suggested by Segal. "Guyana's need for the West Indies is increased by its frontier dispute with Venezuela," he noted. "The Guyanese government is perhaps in a position to trade preferential access to its internal market for certain consumer non-durables not produced in Guyana for West Indian political and economic support."[19]

It is doubtless that any such *quid pro quo* took place in a formal sense, but nonetheless Guyana's increased solidarity with the Commonwealth Caribbean and through it with the third world may have helped to convince Venezuela that she would be paying a price not earlier anticipated if she acted in too aggressive a fashion. The heads of government for the region in their conference at Port of Spain, Trinidad, in February 1969, expressed their "grave concern over the threats posed to Guyana's territorial integrity," and over "the most recent instances of interference in her internal affairs."[20] The conference also stated it

> considered that this situation constituted a serious danger to the peace of the area and deplored any action of an aggressive or hostile nature calculated to further endanger a peaceful resolution of outstanding difficulties. Participating Governments pledged to do all in their power to ensure a settlement of the controversy by peaceful means and in accordance with agreed procedures.[21]

It is not entirely irrelevant that the June 1970 protocol shelving the Venezuela border dispute for twelve years was signed in Port of Spain, Trinidad. Not long before this, in February 1970, Trinidad's Prime Minister Eric Williams had stated in Caracas, in an address to the Inter-American Economic and Social Council, with apparent reference to Guyana's inability at the time to participate in the Organization of American States and Inter-American Development Bank because of the Venezuela claim, that "Guyana's economic development must not be delayed because outstanding differences have not yet been resolved with justice and equity to all concerned."[22] Earlier the *Trinidad Guardian,* reporting on four days of consultations by Trinidad's ambassador to Caracas with Prime Minister Eric Williams and his minister of external affairs, stated that "Trinidad and Tobago is maintaining a close watch on this situation revolving around the recent flare-up in the Guyana-Venezuela border dispute."[23] Minister of State S.S. Ramphal of Guyana and Venezuela's Foreign Minister Aristides Calvani, in the final paragraph of their joint communique in connection with the signing of the June 1970 protocol, took note of the involvement of Williams and his government in achieving the agreement, stating:

> The Ministers recalled that the initial conversations at official level were held in Tobago in March 1970. They expressed their gratitude to the Government of Trinidad and Tobago for their co-operation and support in the holding of these conversations and for the excellence of the facilities provided for the holding of the ministerial meeting in Port-of-Spain. The Ministers placed on record their particular appreciation of the personal efforts of the Prime Minister of Trinidad and Tobago, the Right Honourable Dr. Eric Williams, P.C., in making it possible for these conversations and discussions to have been held with such satisfactory results.[24]

As to decolonization, Burnham has posited a direct relationship between regional integration and achieving economic independence from metropolitan powers, declaring:

> Some of our brothers who still remain our brothers shy away from deciding on a common external tariff and a regionally consistent policy on industrialization and foreign investments. When we were colonies we were politically divided and had all our economic strings tied to the "Mother Country." Now that we are politically independent, it is for us to see that we are not divided for easier foreign economic exploitation. We must substitute a Caribbean orientation for a North American or European one. "Good boys" earn no respect; they are tools to be discarded when dulled by use.[25]

A year earlier, at the April 1970 conference of heads of government of the Commonwealth Caribbean, Burnham, with apparent specific reference to the "black power" revolt then unfolding against "white," or British, and North American domination of Trinidad and Tobago's economy, stated:

> The young and the not so young are not satisfied merely with the fine weather that God has blessed our part of the world with. They are concerned with who owns what in the Caribbean. Some of them say we only own ourselves and even that is subject to question. They are concerned about the ownership and control of the resources of the Caribbean. Let us not be like the proverbial ostrich; and let us recognise that Independence would have been achieved in vain if we do not take regional action, group action with respect to the ownership and control of the resources of the Region.
>
> Some of us are tired of attempting to sing our songs in what has been, in fact, a foreign land. The time has come for us as leaders of our people, as men who have sprung from the gutter, as men who cannot trace their genealogies further than slavery and the proletariat, the time has come for us to give political independence a new turn, for us to achieve economic independence in our part of the world.[26]

Burnham also took the position that Britain's continued presence in the Commonwealth Caribbean, through its responsibility for defense and foreign affairs of the associated states, warranted concern on the part of the region's heads of government. In the address just referred to, he stated:

> I wonder whether it is not our duty at this Conference to take a serious look at the continued and ambivalent presence of the metropolitan power in this region.

> At the United Nations we are sometimes hard put to explain the peculiar constitutional arrangements of the Associated States and sometimes we are concerned by the thin line which divides local rule from external affairs. Maybe the time has come for us as a group, without treading on each other's toes, to re-examine the rationale of the continued British presence in our region as a sovereign power.[27]

The April 1970 heads of government conference made several decisions in line with Burnham's decolonization theme. A resolution was adopted directing the Caribbean Secretariat to convene a joint consultative committee to "examine the present policies in those areas of economic development in which the interests of the people of the Commonwealth Caribbean are not secured" and to "take immediate steps to arrange joint consultation to coordinate policies on land ownership, subdivision and development by foreign interests with a view to establishing machinery to carry out national development of land resources in suitable areas of development with the national interests being secured."[28]

The conference also expressed support for a resolution which had been submitted to the Fourth Committee of the United Nations General Assembly which "recognised that the Constitutions of the Associated States permit their people to proceed to independence (as separate States or in association among themselves or in an association with other independent states in the Region) and recommended that the General Assembly should support any measures taken by the Associated States, in exercise of these options to terminate their relationship with the United Kingdom."[29]

In addition, the conference dealt with mass communications in the region, noting that "the development of a Caribbean consciousness is significantly influenced by the policies pursued" by mass media and that "the policies of foreign or foreign-owned mass media have contributed little to the development of such consciousness." The conference accordingly called for steps toward possible "participation of Governments and West Indian-controlled mass media in the Region, in the management and ownership" of a proposed regional news service.

While Burnham, in achieving power for himself and his party outside a coalition in 1968 and in continuing this unshared power in 1973, did not rely on immigration from the region to Guyana or political integration with one or more regional units, this approach cannot be ruled out for the future. Neither the original mini-CARIFTA agreement of 1965 nor the 1968 agreement provided for free migration in the region. However, the agreements assuredly did not impair the right of a member to admit immigrants from any quarter. There has, in fact, been some movement from the region into Guyana, but apparently not in very significant numbers so far.[30]

Burnham had denied, in defending the political integration proposed by the Grenada Declaration, that he was motivated by electoral considerations. Speaking in a lecture series at the Critchlow Labour College in Georgetown in November 1971 he had stated:

> We are not involved in an attempt to perpetuate the present Governments of signatory and participating territories (that is an internal matter for them). The founding of a West Indian Nation cannot guarantee the survival of the present Governments of any of the territories. They either save themselves or they don't remain, as simple as that.
>
> I am not seeking a West Indian nation to keep me in office, I have other means. I would say further, that though my own political views and orientation are pretty well known as well as those of my Government, what we are involved in at the moment is not the question of getting together people, but in bringing together the territories into a nation or state. The territories having got into a nation, philosophical, ideological and party alignments then will flow freely. . . .
>
> If the state is to be established, naturally my party will seek alignment with such political groups or forces as it considers socialist, and I think that we ought to make this keen distinction between the establishment of the state and the sharing of political and ideological goals and ideals between the respective Governments of the moment in the various territories. It seems to me that this is the context in which we must think, in which we must argue, in which we must propose.[31]

On the other hand, Burnham held the opinion that regional integration was essential for the exercise of any political power worth having. In August 1967, he declared:

> Either we weld ourselves into a regional grouping serving primarily Caribbean needs, or lacking a common positive policy, have our various territories and nations drawn hither and thither into, and by, other large groupings where the peculiar problems of the Caribbean are lost and where we become the objects of neo-colonialist exploitation, and achieve the pitiable status of mendicants.[32]

Again, in November 1971, he stated:

> It seems that, basically, for the West Indies there are only two

alternatives—we either move to union, to unity, or we perish as a people.

We may continue to breathe, we may continue to live, we may continue to move, but we will not be our own masters! We will be dependent upon the generosity of others and since the week has six weekdays and only one Sunday, we must remember the generosity that Christ preaches does not motivate the actions of nations.[33]

Toward the end of the post-independence decade, some of the economic benefits of regional ties seemed to be coming Guyana's way. With the 1973 world oil price hikes, Trinidad's resources and refining capabilities and resulting improved financial capacities became assets that redounded to the benefit of Guyana and other CARICOM members (particularly Jamaica). Further, the regional grouping doubtless provided "strength through numbers" for the important negotiations on economic relations with the European Common Market necessitated by Britain's EEC entry. Finally, Guyana's potential for increased food production and food exportation was enhanced with adoption of a regional food plan under which she has a key role.[34]

However, interestingly enough, during the period when tangible economic benefits seemed to be increasing for Guyana, regional integration did not appear to figure as prominently in Burnham's speeches. It is notable that in two of his major addresses at People's National Congress gatherings, that of December 1974 marking ten years of the PNC in government and that of August 1975 at the party's first biennial congress, integration efforts go unmentioned.[35] Jagan and the PPP, on the other hand, continued their critical position.[36] Further, Clive Thomas, in an article published in the journal of the Ratoon group in 1975 (the year that group joined with others to form the Working People's Alliance), advanced additional criticism under the title "Neo-Colonialism and Caribbean Integration."[37]

It is probable that Burnham, as of the end of the post-independence decade, had found that regional integration had delivered most of the political benefits likely to be obtained from it for some time. His key role, along with that of Attorney General and Foreign Minister S.S. Ramphal, in raising from the ashes of a shattered West Indies Federation the phoenix of a New Commonwealth Caribbean had doubtless enhanced his stature, locally, regionally and even beyond that area. The border disputes were for the time being of much less urgent concern. The region had served an important purpose in Guyana's expanding international involvements, in a sense bridging from the nation's isolation on the South American coast and its colonial and neo-colonial ties to a new role of nonaligned involvement. A different time frame presented different priorities, different imperatives. Without turning from the Commonwealth Caribbean, in fact increasingly meshed with it in important functional and economic respects, Guyana was now playing a role not so much in the region as in the world.

Chapter 4

Obtaining Territorial Control

Coming into independence with some two-thirds of its inherited area under claim by Venezuela and Surinam, and with sparse population in most of the regions affected, it was imperative that Guyana give immediate attention to both legal and physical defense of its territory.

Venezuela's claim is based upon the assertion that Britain, as successor to the Dutch, never got good title to lands west of the Essequibo River. According to this view, the area belonged to Spain, with Venezuela succeeding to that nation's title after its successful independence struggle. The dispute was the subject of a famous arbitration, resulting in an award in 1899 which did not give the British all they claimed to be entitled to, but fell far short of confirming Venezuela's assertion that the Essequibo River should be the boundary. The award was accepted by both parties and the boundary established in accordance with it. The dispute seemed over until in 1949 a memorandum of Severe Mallet-Prevost, who had served as a lawyer for Venezuela in the arbitration proceedings, was published posthumously in the *American Journal of International Law*.[1] The memorandum raised the assertion that a "deal," the dimensions of which were not spelled out, had been made between Russia (a Russian judge had been brought into the dispute as the "neutral" arbitrator) and Britain under which the Russian judge would decide unfavorably, at least in part, to Venezuela's position.

Commenting on the "deal" allegation and Great Britain's defense of the arbitration award after Venezuela had raised the issue in the United Nations, Basil Ince has stated:

> In refuting Mallet-Prevost's implication that there was a "deal" between Great Britain and Russia, the U.K. representative may be on firmer ground since, if there was a deal, nobody had been able to point out what the Russians had gained. The U.K. delegate also contended that at that particular juncture relations between Britain and Russia were strained. A rigid adherent to Marxist philosophy might be quick to point out that there was no need for any deal

between the U.K. and [Russia] to have acted in concert, since they were both imperialist powers, especially in their dealings vis-à-vis colonies and weak states.[2]

Venezuela did little about the matter until in 1962, as Guyana moved toward independence, it raised its claim in debate in the United Nations. Britain asserted that the matter was long settled but permitted Venezuela to look over various pertinent records. Venezuela continued to push the claim and eventually, in February 1966, on the eve of Guyana's independence, an agreement was entered into in Geneva, Switzerland, between the governments of Great Britain, Venezuela, and British Guiana establishing a Mixed Commission. Under the agreement, representatives of British Guiana and Venezuela were to meet from time to time to seek a settlement of the dispute, and, failing settlement within four years of the date of the agreement, the governments of Guyana and Venezuela were to choose one of the means for settlement of disputes set out in Article 33 of the United Nations Charter. Failing agreement on that, they were to refer the decision on settlement "to an appropriate international organ upon which they both agree or, failing agreement on this point, to the Secretary-General of the United Nations."[3]

Mixed commission meetings came and went without resolution of the conflict, and there was a certain amount of military, diplomatic, and international legal skirmishing. Finally, in June 1970, after the four-year period had run out, a protocol to the 1966 Geneva agreement was entered into at Port of Spain, Trinidad, in which it was agreed that for a minimum period of twelve years Venezuela would not assert any claim to sovereignty over the disputed territory and Guyana would not assert a claim to Venezuelan territory.[4] In the meantime, Venezuela and Guyana were to "explore all possibilities of better understanding between them" and to "undertake periodic reviews, through normal diplomatic channels, of their relations, with a view to promoting their improvement and with the aim of producing a constructive advancement of the same."[5]

The Surinam boundary dispute dates from the time of the British-Venezuelan arbitration. The Corentyne River, a broad river running North into the Atlantic Ocean, has been accepted historically as the boundary between British Guiana and Surinam. However, in its upper (southerly) reaches, the river is fed by two main branches The British had taken the position that the easterly branch was the true Corentyne and that their territory comprised everything west of it. The Dutch, however, at the turn of the century, asserted that what the British called the New River, the westerly branch, was the true Corentyne. The land between the branches, known in Guyana as the "New River Triangle," was and is sparsely settled, but it has been thought from time to time that it might hold valuable mineral or petroleum deposits. About 7,000 square miles of territory are involved.

Negotiations between the Dutch and British to settle the matter (and a related question as to whether the boundary between the territories from the Atlantic Ocean southward should be the middle of the Corentyne or the east or west bank) took place during the 1930's but did not result in any final agreement before the advent of World War II. Eventually, in 1962, the same year Venezuela began reasserting its claim to a huge portion of Guyana in earnest, the Netherlands government, on behalf of Surinam, sought to reopen boundary discussions. In April 1966, on the eve of Guyana's independence, the then Surinam leader (formally titled Minister-President) Johannes Pengel declared that "in view of the forthcoming independence of British Guiana, the Surinam Government wishes the British to make it clear when sovereignty was transferred that the frontier is disputed."[6] In June 1966 talks were held in London between representatives of the governments of Guyana, the Netherlands and Surinam with regard to the dispute.

Commenting on the 1966 talks, Prime Minister Burnham asserted in 1969 that the talks

> were held . . . on the understanding that the next invitation would be forthcoming from the Dutch and/or Surinamers. No such invitation has yet been forthcoming in spite of a letter from me to Mr. Pengel, then Minister-President of Surinam, on the 14th September, 1968.[7]

While the Surinam border dispute never assumed the diplomatic or military dimensions of the Venezuela dispute, there were recriminations and some physical conflict (in the New River Triangle)[8] until in April 1970 Prime Minister Burnham and Surinam's Minister-President, Dr. Jules Sedney, meeting in Trinidad "agreed in principal that there should be an early demilitarisation of the border area of Guyana and Surinam in the region of the Upper Corentyne and to the promotion of practical co-operation between Guyana and Surinam in the economic and cultural fields."[9] Working parties of the governments were, under the agreement, to be established to promote plans for implementing the proposals, following which there would be a further meeting of the leaders. It was further agreed that "the discussions between the parties which began in London in 1966 should be resumed in the then existing spirit."[10]

Following meetings of the working parties in Georgetown and Paramaribo in June 1970, Dr. Sedney visited Georgetown June 24 - 27 of that year and the two leaders issued a joint declaration agreeing to immediate demilitarization of the Upper Corentyne region and to "place on a permanent basis the joint examination of ways and means of effecting co-operation in matters of common interest between Surinam and Guyana in the economic, social and cultural fields, and of peacefully resolving all outstanding difficulties and situations which might endanger friendship and good neighborliness between the two countries."[11] To this end, a standing Surinam/Guyana Commission was established, a special committee of which was charged with the responsibility of "continuing the discussions which were adjourned in London in June 1966" and to "exercise fact-finding functions in relation to sources of disharmony in the region of the Upper Corentyne with a view to ensuring that such situations do not disturb friendly relations between the two Governments or prejudice the effective operation of programmes of co-operation agreed upon."[12] The leaders further stated that "in the resolution of all problems between them there shall be resort only to peaceful means and machinery of settlement."[13]

Burnham reciprocated Sedney's visit by spending five days in Surinam in November 1970, at which time the two leaders noted with satisfaction that demilitarization of the Upper Corentyne border area had been effected, approved the text of an agreement for the establishment of a Guyana-Surinam Commission, and announced appointment of its members.[14] The accord's scope and intent were summarized in a preambular expression of desire to "strengthen the historical and traditional bonds of friendship between Guyana and Surinam by active cooperation in the spheres of economic, social and cultural development and by the resolute pursuit of all practical means for the peaceful settlement of difficulties.[15] Similarities between the two polities were recognized in the agreement's preamble, which declared that "in addition to the bonds of geography, Guyana and Surinam have a similar historical and cultural background and possess similar natural resources and economic potential, to the accelerated development of which each Government is committed."[16]

Guyana's border with Brazil, running some 720 miles, is in fact substantially longer than that with either Venezuela or Surinam. Thus it is a matter of considerable good fortune for the nation that it did not face a dispute with Brazil while contending with other neighbors. A treaty of arbitration had been concluded between Britain and Brazil in 1901. An award was given in 1904 and the actual demarcation of the British Guiana frontier carried out in the 1930's.[17]

Guyana and Brazil had cordial relations during most of the post-independence decade. As a result of a mission to Rio de Janeiro and Brazilia by a Guyanese party headed by Minister of State and Attorney General S.S. Ramphal in August 1969, a program of technical cooperation was initiated by Brazil's embassy in Georgetown. In October 1969 two senior officers of the Guyana Defence Force began training at Manaus, Brazil at the Instruction

Center for Jungle Warfare. Also in October of that year, the well-known Brazilian anthropologist Gilberto Freyre visited Guyana and gave the inaugural lecture in the University of Guyana's new lecture hall.

Visiting Guyana in January 1970, the managing editor of *The Daily Journal* of Caracas concluded, after interviews with Burnham and Ramphal, that "In analyzing the Brazilian presence it is clear that more than anything else Guyana expects to counter the giant that is Venezuela with another giant." He quotes Ramphal as stating that "We found the Brazilians genuinely interested in helping us and not in trying to dispute territories. They are champions of settled frontiers." Burnham asserted that "One can only go on evidence, and that shows that Brazil has no intention to usurp our territory."[19]

The Venezuela and Surinam claims had a positive side, from the viewpoint of the Burnham-led government, in that they provided an opportunity to employ the classic device of appealing for national unity in the face of external threats. The fact that elites of Venezuela could be imaged as "European" or "white," in contrast to the preponderant population of Guyana, could only enhance the positive impact on national unity. The claims also enhanced decolonization by tending to inhibit foreign investment in Guyana, particularly in the portion under claim by Venezuela, some five-eighths of the total land area. The lack of any substantial backing from Britain or the United States for Guyana in dealing with the claims doubtless influenced the Burnham government toward a quest for support from Commonwealth Caribbean and other third world polities, a relational shift further enhancing decolonization.

Admittedly, dealing with the border claims did result in considerable diversion of resources and governmental attention from tasks of economic and social development. Then too, the Venezuelan claim was related to the Rapununi uprising of January 1969, a traumatic event in the life of the young nation. However, the claims, and the uprising as well, gave an impetus to opening up and settling the nation's interior or "hinterland," as well as to the related task of strengthening bonds between the interior-dwelling Amerindians and the balance of Guyanese society. Further, the claims necessitated a mobilization of national resources in a number of fields which, once attention could be shifted from the external threats, could be turned to social and economic development tasks.

Burnham's strongest pleas for national unity came after the Rupununi uprising of January 1969 raised grave questions regarding his government's ability to hold the loyalties of the nation's citizenry, especially those in remote hinterland areas. The Rupununi revolt involved ranchers and Amerindians of that area, near the Brazil border but within territory claimed by Venezuela. Venezuela was implicated in training and equipping the participants.[20] The incident also cast suspicions, however unfounded, on United Force party leader Peter d'Aguiar, who had visited the area bearing details of the December 1968 election to his constituents (who predominated there, as in much of the interior) prior to the incident.[21]

Speaking at a mass meeting in Georgetown in May 1969, Burnham reminded his listeners of the uprising earlier that year, which, he asserted, "was encouraged and which was connived by Venezuela," and quoted John Jay's assertion (1787) that "weakness and divisions at home would invite dangers from abroad."[22] In a speech to an Aid Donors Conference in Georgetown in September 1969, he likened Guyana's position to that of Job, declaring that "To the west there is Venezuela, to the east there is Surinam and to the north there is the sea."[23]

Some months after Venezuelan Foreign Minister Aristides Calvani had accused the Burnham government of "setting up a racial government in the heart of Latin America,"[24] and after a Venezuelan Foreign Ministry spokesman had asserted, in reference to Guyana's expulsion of a Surinam force from territory claimed by that country, that "Venezuela follows with growing concern the aggressive movements of Guyana, which jointly with the racist policies of Prime Minister Burnham may seriously disturb the peace in the Latin American continent,"[25] Burnham turned the racial allegation back toward Venezuela. Speaking at the annual conference of his People's National Congress in April 1970, he puzzled over Venezuela's motives in pursuing the territorial claim with the following words:

> When one considers the size of Venezuela, its wealth and its thousands of square miles of undeveloped land (more than the whole of Guyana) one finds it impossible to square its avarice with its oft repeated intentions and love for freedom. Can it be that the mineral wealth of Essequibo excites this avarice? Can it be that the fact that ours is the only non-white republic on the American continent explains it? Why do the Venezuelan leaders seek to subvert the Amerindian section of our population? Why do they, with their problems of guerillas, university violence, assassination of the brother of a Foreign Minister, seek to suggest that we are seeking to create diversions to turn attention from our internal problems—problems which are miniscule as compared to theirs? We have no territorial ambitions, we want to rule no one but ourselves. All we ask is to be allowed to develop in peace and without interference from outside, our Guyana for ourselves.[26]

In one sense, Burnham had a clear and smooth path in using the territorial claims to orchestrate national unity. The necessity for defense of territorial integrity was a matter on which none of the major political parties or figures did, or could afford to, disagree. Speaking as premier, Jagan had declared in a

1964 Legislative Assembly address that "The Government of British Guiana is not prepared to yield to Venezuela or to any other country a single rivulet or creek; we are not prepared to surrender a single inch of the soil of this country."[27] The United Force party likewise insisted on defense of territorial integrity. R.E. Cheeks, a United Force minister in the coalition government, stated during the July 1968 National Assembly debate on Guyana-Venezuela relations:

> I should like the Venezuelans and the world to know that we in Guyana here are not prepared to expose our freedom and will not be the ones to expose our continent to any danger from outside. The eyes of the world are on us and Venezuelans must appear like the bullies that they are. They behaved with circumspection while the imperial power ruled here. As soon as we got our sovereignty they have begun to rattle their war drums and apparently wish to move in on us.[28]

However, when it came to the diplomatic and legal strategies for opposing the claims, the PPP's position was hardly lockstepped with that of the PNC-UF coalition government, or with the PNC government after the coalition's termination. Whereas the PNC-UF coalition willingly entered into the Geneva Agreement of February 1966 establishing a mixed commission "with the task of seeking satisfactory solutions for the practical settlement of the controversy between Venezuela and the United Kingdom which has arisen as the result of the Venezuelan contention that the Arbitral Award of 1899 about the frontier between British Guiana and Venezuela is null and void"[29] and, after independence, participated in extensive deliberations with Venezuela in the Mixed Commission, the PPP took the position that since Venezuela's claim had no substance, the Mixed Commission should never have been established.

Jagan, in his statement in the July 1968 National Assembly debate on Guyanese-Venezuelan relations, asserted that "the Venezuelan Government today is the puppet of the Government of the United States of America"[30] and charged that the United States, Great Britain, and Venezuela were involved in a conspiracy to prevent the PPP from regaining power in Guyana,[31] He then asked:

> Why was it necessary for the Government to sign the Geneva Agreements? Why did the British Government which, in our time, said that the matter was closed, agree to the reopening of the question at Geneva? Was it not to allow the Venezuelans to keep this question going, to be examined by a Mixed Commission until perhaps another election came along, which the PPP might win, fraud or no fraud?[32]

People's Progressive Party objections to the Guyana government's handling of the Venezuela claim continued after the signing of the June 1970 Port of Spain protocol in which the two countries agreed to shelve the claim for some twelve years. Jagan declared shortly after the signing of the agreement was announced that "The Geneva Agreement was part of the Anglo-American conspiracy to maintain Guyana as a neo-colonial state. The Trinidad Protocol is another step in the same direction."[33] In the National Assembly debate on the shelving agreement, he asserted that

> not only the P.P.P., but the man in the street wants to have this issue settled once and for all . . . . When the people are under pressure here, something is going to happen on the border to deflect attention from the problems at home. And when the Venezuelan Government has pressures, we will have incidents on the border. . . .
>
> The people of this country demand that this issue be settled and this matter should be taken to the Secretary-General of the United Nations with the recommendation that it should be referred if necessary to the World Court.[34]

Some evidence that the border disputes had in fact enhanced national identity was provided in a government white paper, "Guyana/Venezuela Relations," issued by the Ministry of External Affairs in September 1968. The paper lists some fifty-four Guyanese organizations, categorized under the headings religious groups, local government bodies, groups of citizens, business and professional groups, trade unions, other voluntary associations, youth groups, and political parties, which had pledged support to the Guyana government in the face of the territorial claims. However, while the Guyana Council of Churches, referred to as representing "13 major Christian denominations," and one village Islamic body were listed under religious groups, Hindu organizations were notable for their absence.[35] This striking omission was rectified in September 1969 when Sase Narain, president of the leading Guyanese Hindu organization, the Maha Sabha, responding to reports that Venezuelan President Rafael Caldera and Foreign Minister Aristides Calvani had described the Guyana government as a racist regime, warned that Venezuelan leaders were "making a serious miscalculation if they believe they could promote their territorial claims by seeking to divide the people of Guyana." He further stated:

> For the purpose of territorial integrity, the Hindus are at one with all in Guyana in defending every square foot of our beloved country and will not be misguided by the divisionist statements by Venezuela for the purpose of promoting its expansionist aims. . . .

> Guyana is a truly multi-racial society. In this context it is ludicrous for the Venezuelan Government to compare Guyana with Venezuela where more than 80 per cent of their population is of one ethnic group as it is to suggest that Venezuela is champion of minority groups in the hemisphere having regard to its own record of mistreatment of its indigenous people."[36]

Venezuelan strategies in pressing their territorial position included placement of an advertisement in the *Times* of London (June 15, 1968) warning potential investors that the Venezuelan government would not recognize concessions granted by the Guyanese government in the disputed area as well as the issuance of a presidential decree (July 9, 1969) stating an intention of exercising jurisdiction over ocean waters within a three-mile strip adjacent to the shore.[37] The Guyanese government protested these moves as a violation of the 1966 Geneva agreement setting up the mixed commission and as contrary to international law.[38] However, there is little doubt that the Venezuelan moves, along with the already unsettled legal situation in the area under dispute, adversely affected foreign investment. Companies either operating in or contemplating operation in Venezuela were presumably especially vulnerable, since should they undertake investments in the claimed territory, they could be subjected to unwelcome pressures in that country. The managing editor of the Caracas English-language paper, the *Daily Journal,* reported following conversations with government officials in Georgetown, that the presidential decree had "paralysed the possible exploration of oil deposits in that area."[39]

The 1970 protocol shelving the border dispute for a minimum of twelve years, involving as it does an understanding by Venezuela not to assert any claim to sovereignty over the territory in dispute, presumably should be interpreted as negating the London Times advertisement and the presidential decree.[40] However, it would seem probable that the permitted revival of the claim after the twelve-year period has expired would have an unsettling effect on the foreign investment climate.

The diversion of resources from development as a result of mobilization to meet the Venezuelan claim was stressed by S.S. Ramphal, then Attorney General and Minister of State, when he addressed the United Nations General Assembly in October 1968. Ramphal, after lamenting continuing Venezuelan pressures, declared:

> Every million dollars that a developing nation spends on defense, whether it be on aircraft or on ships or on a standing army, or on any of their several adjuncts, represents a million dollars diverted from development. Indeed, in some cases, it may represent a much

> greater diversion—dependent on the terms of bilateral or multilateral assistance available to the State for projects of development.
>
> And this is to say nothing of the diversions of human resources, of expertise, of manpower, of energies from the urgent tasks of social and economic change to which they ought to be applied.[41]

Doubtless some of the diverted resources that Ramphal was referring to went into interior development and thus are not lost in terms of the nation's long-term growth. Hinterland development was spurred by the awareness, resulting from the January 1969 Rupununi uprising, that loyalties and control in the interior could not be taken for granted. Burnham asserted in August 1969 that his call, in May of that year, for movement into the interior had met with "an enthusiastic response from the young people of Guyana." He declared that the purpose of relocation was two-fold. People were being sent "to make a living and to provide an important line of defense against attack on our borders."[42]

Hubert Jack, then a government minister without portfolio, presented the relationships between the territorial claims and interior development succinctly in his speech at the April 1970 PNC annual conference, asserting:

> We must consider also the question of the nation's security. We live on the narrow coastal strip and our neighbors both on the east and on the west have laid claims, as you know, to large tracts of land. In many cases, though this land is ours, it is largely uninhabited. This situation must be redressed as quickly as possible.[43]

Hinterland settlement does not come naturally for most Guyanese, and it is doubtful if, without the impetus of the land dispute, any very substantial interior development would have occurred for some time. Burnham had asked, in his report to the nation on the first anniversary of Independence, May 1967:

> But how long will we remain huddled on a coastal strip when the vast resources of our hinterland cry out for exploitation? Our mighty rivers are ready to yield up their wealth of diamonds and precious stones and teem with fish for food. Our rich riverain lands in the interior lie idle and unscratched. The extent of our mineral reserves have only been guessed.[44]

Two years later, on the third anniversary of independence, Burnham asserted:

> We cannot allow our rich hinterland to remain almost uninhabited and uncultivated. The sight of these rich lands lying unexploited

tends to excite the avarice of some covetous souls and to encourage the vaulting ambitions of others. We must possess these lands. To this end government is formulating plans for the orderly development of the interior. The Interior Development Committee is expected to hand in its report by July and thereafter speedy action will be taken to set up the necessary machinery for the settlement and development of our vast inland areas. In this development every Guyanese (without exception) will have a fair and just share.[45]

The commitment to hinterland development is manifested in the nation's second development plan, covering the period 1972-76, with allocations for road, food processing, leather working, and agricultural projects in several interior regions.[46] Further, the National Service program put forward in December 1973 places considerable emphasis on interior development. The State Paper outlining the program asserts that "New agricultural townships in the Hinterlands are expected to be established as a necessary and complementary part of National Service Training." The Paper also declared that "Service with the Pioneer Corps [a one-year period of training for all Guyanese between the ages of 18 and 25] will be a prerequisite for the settlement of young people on State-owned or Government-owned lands in the hinterland."[47]

Attention to integration of the Amerindians into national society has of necessity been parallel with concern for interior development as a means of securing and controlling the nation's inherited territory. Numbering only approximately 32,000 as of 1968 and constituting about 4.5% of the nation's population, the Amerindians live almost entirely in the interior.[48] Relations between them and the coastal-dwelling Guyanese have been clouded by memories of their employment in times past by slave owners to track down escapees.[49]

A number of Amerindians were involved with ranchers in the aborted January 1969 Rupununi uprising. Prime Minister Burnham, in his broadcast report to the nation on the uprising, asserted that

> The insurrection as we know was planned, organised and carried out by the ranchers of the Rupununi—the savannah aristocrats. Such Amerindian citizens as were involved were employed in a secondary capacity and appeared generally to have acted under duress and in response to the orders of their rancher employers. Nevertheless, within a few hours of the attack on Lethem, the Venezuelan press and radio were reporting an Amerindian uprising in the Rupununi and suggesting that it arose out of the wish of these Guyanese citizens to come under the sovereignty of Venezuela.[50]

Some six months earlier, in the National Assembly debate on Guyana-Venezuela relations, R.E. Cheeks, of the United Force party, Minister of Local Government in the coalition government, had declared:

> But Venezuela appears to be interfering in our domestic affairs at another level, sir. They are at present seeking to subvert people who live in the interior on our border. I am just from there. At present there are Guyanese Amerindians who are being encouraged to go across to Venezuela to enjoy benefits which are not enjoyed by the Venezuelan Amerindians themselves. They are being induced to cross the border and are being given free books, free food, free lodgings, in fact, free everything. The Venezuelans are doing this thing clandestinely.[51]

Guyana's independence constitution contained a special annex intended to protect Amerindian rights in lands on which they were settled and stating a policy of assisting them "to the stage where they can, without disadvantage to themselves, be integrated with the rest of the community."[52] Under the constitutional provision, a Commission was to be established after independence to determine how lands should be allocated. The Commission was established in September 1967 but had not completed its report as of the time of the Rupununi revolt. The uprising, as well as other imperatives for assuring Amerindian loyalties in the face of the Venezuela position, spurred the government into action, and a conference of Amerindian leaders was held in Georgetown in late February and early March of 1969, resulting in a number of governmental undertakings in the fields of road construction, agricultural assistance, health and education.

The Lands Commission completed its report in August 1969, but the report was neither approved nor made public until the eve of conversion to Republic status, February 1970. By that time some Amerindians, wary that with Guyana as a Republic they might lose protections contained in the independence constitution, had petitioned the government for action.[53] It was also reported from Caracas that many Amerindians were crossing the border into Venezuela.[54]

The Lands Commission report was made available finally at a four-day conference of Indian leaders in Georgetown which commenced February 6, 1970.[55] At the opening session Burnham announced the creation of a buffer zone some ten miles in depth along the nation's frontiers within which no one, Amerindian or other, would be granted legal title to occupy lands and within which no occupation would be permitted without governmental approval.[56] Although assuring the Amerindians of his government's willingness to resolve the lands issue, Burnham intimated at the opening session that he was aware of Amerindian movements across the Venezuela border and, according to the

Guyana Graphic, warned that while there was no plan to restrict or deny the rights of Amerindians, as part of the Guyanese nation they must understand that their first loyalty was to Guyana.[57]

At the conclusion of the conference, the Amerindian leaders accepted the Lands Commission report, with a few modifications, and pledged loyalty and allegiance to the government and state of Guyana. The government had enunciated a policy during the conference of granting legal title on a communal basis rather than to individual Amerindians.

Actual passage of title to lands did not take place until April 1976, shortly before the tenth anniversary of independence. Certificates covering some 4,500 square miles were turned over to sixty-one Amerindian communities at a meeting of chiefs, leaders and delegates in Georgetown, with the promise of future transfer of more land.[58] Under legislation adopted by the National Assembly in this connection, the conveyances are subject to a number of restrictions, including government retention of title to rivers, mineral and mining rights, and existing airstrips. Provision for loss of title is made where members of the community on whose behalf title is held "have shown themselves by act or speech to be disloyal or disaffected towards the State or have done any voluntary act which is incompatible with their loyalty to the State."[59] According to one report, the total lands to be conveyed amount to some 9,000 square miles.[60] With regard to earlier Amerindian hopes for receiving some 43,000 of the nation's 83,000 square miles, Prime Minister Burnham is reported to have stated in the April 1976 meeting of chiefs and others, "Let's be realistic. All of us have to live here, and it would be a joke if 40,000 of the population of over 700,000 were to get more than half of the land space."[61]

One element of the governmental machinery which the border disputes have doubtless enhanced, especially in training and experience, is the Guyana Defense Force. Its size as of February 1970 was put at 1600 men by the Caracas *Daily Journal* managing editor then visiting Georgetown.[62] The *Daily Journal's* correspondent regarded the GDF as a "highly trained force, carried out by British officers with experience in Malaysia and by Brazilians."[63] He noted that additionally there were some 2500 men in the police force.

The Defence Force was assigned substantial responsibilities in the nation's Second Development Plan, 1972-76. The plan, in a chapter titled "The Role of the Army," noted that "Since the establishment of the Guyana Defence Force in 1966, the scope of its operation has grown considerably from conventional activities pertaining to the preservation of national security, to a significant involvement in every aspect of national development."[64]

According to the Development Plan, "the Army will continue to establish and run large-scale farms in several regions throughout the country."[65] The Plan emphasizes the "pioneering and leadership role that the Army will be required to assume in the thrust towards the development of the hinterland," and states:

> The Engineering Command will be directly responsible for the construction of hinterland roads and bridges, the upgrading of airstrips and projects such as the rehabilitation of the hydroelectric power station at Tumatumari [a small-scale generator]. The training of farmers/settlers in the Farm Corps will be done on location in the hinterland. The Army's airwing and telecommunication services will be available to hinterland communities in cases of emergency, while its Medical Corps will at all times be on call to civilians wherever the need exists.[66]

Undoubtedly the single most significant interior development project undertaken during the first decade of independence involves a major hydroelectric project on the Upper Mazaruni River, deep within the area claimed by Venezuela. In 1972 a Yugoslavian firm, Energo Projekt, undertook prefeasibility studies. The Swedish engineering consultant firm SWECO, A.B. was retained in mid-1975 and has had continued involvement since then. Construction of a 188-mile access road was begun in February 1975. Guyana Defence Force personnel have cooperated on the road aspect. Planned capacity of the system's generators is estimated at 1,000 megawatts, with eventual increase to 3,000 megawatts. Construction of a 225,000-ton aluminum smelter is envisaged, presumably at Linden, the nation's key bauxite center, with power transmitted to that location as well as elsewhere for industrial, agricultural and other uses. Overall, it is estimated the project will cost three billion Guyana dollars.[67]

Thus, Guyana ended its first decade of nationhood with legal and physical control of territory on a substantially firmer footing than at independence. Relations with Brazil and Venezuela had become more turbulent near the end of the decade, as will be detailed in a later chapter, but the border disputes remained "on the shelf." Important progress had been made in assuring support from the Amerindians and in more completely possessing and utilizing the country's vast interior expanses.

Chapter 5

From Western Alignment to Nonalignment

> Whether by choice or necessity, the Commonwealth Caribbean states have committed themselves fully to the western world. In the entire Commonwealth Caribbean, the only dogmatically anti-western political force of some significance is Cheddi Jagan's People's Progressive Party of Guyana, which has been relegated into opposition since 1964. . . .[1]

In the spring of 1969, when Roy Preiswerk expressed this view of alignments of Guyana and other Commonwealth Caribbean states, it seemed to be a reasonably accurate summary. Since then, Guyana has moved toward or into a neutralist stance, becoming an active participant in the nonaligned movement, diminishing the intensity of its relationships with western capitalist states and establishing closer ties with communist nations.

When the Burnham-led People's National Congress-United Force coalition government came into office in December 1964, it succeeded People's Progressive Party leadership which had sought ties with the Castro government in Cuba as well as with the Soviet Union and Eastern European states. Rice sales to Cuba and the U.S.S.R. had resulted, and Cuba provided oil at the critical point when the regular supplies were cut during the 1963 general strike.[2]

After discussions between Dr. Jagan and Dr. Ernesto (Che) Guevara in 1960 and 1961, the Cuban government offered substantial loans, involving provision of equipment and materials for development of a hydro-electric project and of funds to assist with a timber and wood-pulp project. Interest was set at 2% and repayment would be out of woodpulp and other timber products.[3] Jagan's government sought to accept a Hungarian proposal, submitted in response to an invitation for competitive bids, to establish a Guyana Government-owned glass factory using West German components. It also negotiated a contract for a rice-bran oil factory with the German Democratic Republic. None of these projects came to fruition, although the rice-bran oil factory agreement was eventually signed in 1964, with the coalition government, according to Jagan, abandoning it after coming into office. Jagan blames British and American resistance for his difficulties in firming up these programs, noting, so far as the Cuban assistance was concerned, that since it fell in the orbit of foreign affairs, the offer had to be referred to the Colonial Office.[4] He asserts that "These steps had been taken after the British government had decided not to assist us. Having failed to defeat us with divide-and-rule methods, terror and manipulated elections, it had embarked on an economic squeeze-play to oust us."[5]

Jagan also recounts efforts to obtain increased United Kingdom assistance as well as United States and World Bank aid. Regarding the October 1961 visit to Washington during which he met with President John F. Kennedy, Jagan states that "In the U.S. capital, I was given the 'glad-hand' treatment by officials of the various U.S. aid agencies, that [sic] nothing tangible materialized."[6] The World Bank eventually lent US $2 million, much less than requested, and specified agricultural, forestry, and fishery use rather than industrialization, which Jagan had sought. Arthur M. Schlesinger, Jr., presents an "inside-the-White-House" view of Jagan's Washington visit and subsequent decisions regarding aid to his government:

> Assuming that Jagan would be the leader of an independent British Guiana, we estimated that, if we gave aid, there would be a fifty per cent chance of his going communist, that, if we didn't, there would be a ninety per cent chance, and that we would all catch hell whatever we did. The State Department at first thought we should make the try; then Rusk personally reversed this policy in a stiff letter to the British early in 1962. AID was fearful from the start that assistance to British Guiana would cause congressional criticism and injure the whole aid programme. The President, after meeting Jagan, had grown increasingly sceptical, but he was impressed by the British contention that there was no alternative. The British advanced this argument at every opportunity, though one always suspected that their main desire was to get out of British Guiana as quickly as possible and dump the whole problem on us (nor could one begrudge the Colonial Office its sarcasm when Americans, after bringing self-righteous pressure on London to advance the independence timetable in Africa, now kept urging delay in this case). Inside British Guiana the situation continued to disintegrate. In February 1962 frightening race riots broke out in Georgetown. Jagan, forgetting his objection to imperialism, requested British troops to help maintain order.[7]

Schlesinger continues his account of the Kennedy administration's dealings with Guyanese affairs by indicating changing official attitudes toward Burnham. The attitudes had been largely negative, based upon British appraisals, but Burnham apparently made a favorable impression in Washington during a May 1962 visit. The conclusion was reached that "an independent British Guiana under Burnham (*if* Burnham will commit himself to a multi-racial policy) would cause us many fewer problems than an independent British Guiana under Jagan," and institution of a proportional representation electoral system was seen as the "obvious solution" in terms of getting Jagan out of power. Citing the establishment of the proportional representation system and the installation of a coalition government under Burnham as a result of the 1964 elections, Schlesinger concludes, "with much unhappiness and turbulence, British Guiana seemed to have passed safely out of the communist orbit."[8]

Whether or not Schlesinger knew it at the time, the United States, through the CIA, had had its part in the "unhappiness and turbulence" experienced within Guyana. Details of CIA financing of trade union activists who sought the Jagan government's ouster, based upon London *Sunday Times* and *New York Times* accounts published in 1967, are presented by Ronald Radosh in his study of the role of labor organizations in U.S. foreign policy:

> The well-known "insight" team from the London *Times* reported in a detailed series that the overthrow of Jagan's government "was engineered largely by the C.I.A." The cover used, they reported, was "A London-based international trades union secretariat, the Public Service International." As coups go, the article continued, "it was not expensive: over five years the CIA paid out something over 250,000 pounds." "For the colony... the result was about 170 dead, untold hundreds wounded, roughly 10 million pounds worth of damage to the economy and a legacy of racial bitterness." But the tool for unseating Jagan's government was "the Guyanese trade union movement"....
>
> Not only did Arnold Zander [president, until 1964, of what Radosh describes as Public Service International's major American affiliate union, the Federation of State, County and Municipal Employees] get CIA money for his Guianese operations, the *New York Times* added, but the CIA, "operating under cover of the American union, helped pro-Burnham dike and public employees unions organize strikes" in 1962 and 1963. "The agents gave advice to local union leaders on how to organize and sustain the strikes," and also provided "funds and food supplies to keep the strikes going and medical supplies for pro-Burnham workers injured during the turmoil. At one point, one of the agents even served as a member of

a bargaining committee from the Guiana workers union that was negotiating with Dr. Jagan." The *Times* estimated that Zander received sixty thousand dollars annually from the CIA until May 1964.[9]

Once the People's National Congress-United Force government was in office, following the December 1964 election, British and American aid prospects were much brighter. Sir Cameron Mitchell has observed that

> As soon as Burnham headed the Guyanese Government, the [Cuban] rice contract was not renewed. The P.N.C. Government obtained increased aid from the United States and Great Britain, while it also stimulated investment from Western countries.[10]

As independence neared, Burnham, in remarks at the diplomatic training course sponsored by Guyana's Ministry of External Affairs in January 1966, attempted to establish a framework in which future evolution of the new nation's international affiliations and loyalties could be understood. He recalled that some five years earlier he had declared that Guyana would be "no pawn of East or West." However, he sought to allay fears that Guyana might serve as a base for aggression against "western" positions or that it lacked a proper sense of gratitude for economic assistance bestowed from that quarter in the months since the People's National Congress-United Force coalition had replaced the People's Progressive Party government. Thus he stated:

> Apart from considerations attendant on the fact of our being geographically situated in the western hemisphere, I have repeatedly stated that we, in Guyana, share with the West its oft-pronounced dedication and firm attachment to the democratic principle. Further, my government will never tolerate the establishment of any military base aimed at aggression against any of our neighbours or any nation in the hemisphere. We have been the recipients of substantial capital and technical assistance from the West, for all of which we are most deeply grateful.[11]

On the other hand, Burnham asserted "all of this does not mean that we automatically support the Western Bloc or any of its members in any action or stand they take on the international scene,"[12] and he proceeded to condemn "kid glove treatment being meted out by Britain and her allies to the renegade and illegal Smith regime in Rhodesia."[13] Turning to the East, he attempted a balanced attitude, declaring that while Guyana's experience with western imperialism must not "lead it to ignore the risks of other imperialisms ... we have got to have such relations as we think will be in the interest of our country and the interest of the community of nations."[14]

After asserting the importance of Caribbean regional integration, Burnham turned to the Afro-Asian group. As if forecasting the close ties Guyana would establish with third world nations once the PNC achieved power outside its coalition with the UF, he stated:

> On the wider scene this government recognises the common bonds which exist between Guyana and the Afro-Asian block. They are not merely the almost accidental ones of ethnic origin, but more important, are traceable to the fact that we all, in common international parlance, are ex-colonial, formerly exploited and euphemistically described as developing nations.
>
> We are all considered potential game for satellite status by the larger nations and we are all at the same time anxious to maintain true independence. The influence and significance of the Afro-Asian block in the Commonwealth and the United Nations must not be underestimated. It is tremendous. The members of this group might not have in the past been successful in achieving all their objectives. But even so which group has? Some of us may be critical, perhaps hypercritical, of the failure of members of that bloc to pass a positive judgment on the Sino-Indian hostilities but no one equates Christianity with Satanic wickedness because of its failure in some instances to give the proper leadership one would have expected of it.
>
> Let us not be brain-washed or cynically and deliberately flattered by the big powers into believing that this third force in the world today is without philosophy, or cohesion and merely the object of manipulation by one or other of the two major power blocs. It represents something new, something dynamic, in international politics. I am convinced that the existence of this group is symbolic of international democracy in that it provides an opportunity for the opinion of the small nation to have equal weight to that of the international Leviathans.[15]

The United States' preference for Burnham's and the coalition government's leadership over that of Jagan and the PPP, hardly a matter of doubt, was alluded to at the time of independence when Lincoln Gordon, U.S. Assistant Secretary of State and head of the U.S. delegation to the independence ceremonies, in presenting Burnham (an avid horseman) with a custom-made western saddle from President Johnson, stated "With it go President Johnson's best wishes, in which we all share, that you may always 'ride tall in the saddle.'"[16] Gordon also participated in the ceremony on Guyana's first day of independence, May 26, 1966, in which an agreement affecting the huge, 17,000 acre Atkinson Field base about twenty miles south of Georgetown was executed. According to a press release issued at the time, under the agreement's terms the U.S "relinquished all claims to Atkinson Field and the land and installations today become the property of the people and the Government of Guyana." However, "Certain contingency rights for the use of Atkinson Field are granted to the United States for a period of 17 years, subject thereafter to termination upon one year's written notice by either party." The contingency rights "include authority for U.S. Government aircraft to overfly Guyana and to use the facilities at Atkinson on a temporary basis. These rights, however, are subject to the advance filing of flight plans and payment for all services rendered."[17]

Even before the independence day Atkinson agreement had actually been signed, Jagan declared with reference to it that "Landing rights in Guyana can facilitate US troop movements not only in South America but also in Africa," asserting that "It is clear that the coalition government has bartered away our sovereignty. It makes a farce of the pronouncement of the Prime Minister that Guyana will remain neutral "[18]

In March 1967, in the first National Assembly debate on foreign policy, Burnham distinguished between "neutrality" and "Neutralism," characterizing the former as cowardly and unrealistic and the latter as involving the independent exercise of judgment on international questions.[19] He asserted that "Guyana does not propose to make itself the protagonist or advocate of one or other of the super powers or blocs."[20] He then placed Guyana with neutralist nations, stating:

> But, sir, there has been what has been called a third bloc. What has been called a third bloc, consists of the neutralist powers or nations.
>
> Guyana belongs to this third group. Most, if not all the members of this group consist of underdeveloped countries or nations. These underdeveloped nations are disappointed that the 'decade of development' starting in 1960, has proved to be a flop so far. It is my belief that these underdeveloped nations can, in spite of their limited resources, develop not only formal political links but trade and economic links, and can come together for their mutual benefits and protection. This can be done especially in cases where they are the sole producers of certain important commodities, goods and or minerals.[21]

Commenting on Burnham's espousal of a neutralist position for Guyana, Jagan stated:

> No one can seriously quarrel with this stand. Guyana, though a small nation, is part of an interdependent world. Our relationships, and thus our foreign policy, must be determined by what we consider to be our national interests and our international obligations.
>
> Where we differ, however, from the coalition government is not on its pronouncement, but on its performance. The government does not practice what it preaches. For public consumption at home and abroad, it says one thing, but does the opposite. While it claims to be non-aligned, it is completely tied to the West, particularly the U.S.A. Washington dictates our foreign policy; she decides with whom we must establish diplomatic contacts, trade and aid links. There is abundant evidence of this.
>
> The agreement on the U.S. military bases in Guyana confers on the U.S. government the right to erect military installations at Atkinson Field and Makouria, to land military equipment and personnel, and to fly over our territory. The U.S.A. trains and equips our police force (direct aid of $500,000 given so far), while its junior partner, Britain, is in command of our military and security forces.[22]

Jagan was also critical of arrangements for the 1966 independence celebrations, remarking "Of the Socialist East, only the USSR and Yugoslavia were invited; [the] People's Republic of China and Cuba were excluded."[23] He continued:

> The inclusion of Chiang-Kai-Shek's government was defended by the Prime Minister on the ground that outside of the Afro-Asian countries only United Nations Security Council members were to be the invitees.
>
> This attempt to cover up dictation from Washington was exposed later when the former Minister of Economic Development, Mr. J. Henry Thomas, paid a visit in early 1966 to Chiang-Kai-Shek's Taiwan, and still later when the Guyana government supported at the United Nations the U.S. "two Chinas" policy, and voted against the People's Republic of China taking her rightful place in the Security Council as the real representative of the people of China.
>
> In keeping with U.S. world-wide diplomatic pressure for the isolation and blockade of Cuba and China (not heeded even by its Western allies, the United Kingdom, France and Canada), the

coalition government had abandoned trade with Cuba and placed serious restrictions on the importation of less costly goods from the socialist countries. Economic aid comes only from the U.K., Canada and West Germany. Offers made publicly by the U.S.S.R. to provide aid, and suggestions for the establishment of trade and diplomatic links have been sidestepped.[24]

Jagan called for "Close links with the countries of the genuinely nonaligned 'third bloc' whose problems and aspirations are not dissimilar and who would play a role in advancing international peace and democratic developments"[25] and concluded:

So long as the United States of America continues to dictate our domestic and foreign policies, the crisis will inevitably deepen. Like De Gaulle's France, it is possible with a progressive foreign policy to postpone the crisis resulting from a reactionary domestic policy. But with a reactionary foreign policy as in Guyana, there can be no progressive domestic policy. The economic crisis can only worsen.[26]

One aspect of Guyana's western linkage was scheduled, under terms of its independence constitution, to continue at least into 1969. The document provided for a "Governor General and Commander-in-Chief of Guyana who shall be appointed by Her Majesty and shall hold office during Her Majesty's pleasure and who shall be Her Majesty's representative in Guyana."[27] However, it also provided that the position of governor general could be replaced by that of a president elected by the National Assembly, if that body so resolved by majority vote of all elected members, upon a motion introduced by the Prime Minister. At least three months notice of the motion was required and the notice could not be given before January 1, 1969.[28]

The constitutional provision regarding delay until after that date for conversion to republic status was apparently adopted as a result of differences between the United Force and the People's National Congress. An introduction to Burnham's remarks in the August 1969 National Assembly debate on change of status, as published in a volume of his collected speeches, states:

At the Constitutional Conference of 1965, Mr. Burnham made clear his intention to make Guyana a constitutional republic as soon as possible after independence was attained. This was resisted by the minority United Force, at that time still a part of Burnham's coalition government. A compromise was reached whereby the independence constitution would provide for Guyana to change from a monarchy to a republic through a simple majority vote in the National Assembly but that such a motion could not be introduced until 1969.[29]

The People's Progressive Party (which had refused to participate in the 1965 constitution conference because a state of emergency continued to exist in Guyana and because a number of persons were under detainment)[30] would have preferred independence without any ties to the British crown. Burnham was thus assured of that party's support in the vote on republic conversion, although by August 1969, when the change was debated in the National Assembly, the People's National Congress had sufficient seats to adopt the necessary resolution, with or without PPP help. The United Force, in its 1968 election campaign literature, had favored continued monarchical status, two of the elements of its instructions for party workers being "Unity under the Queen" and "No Republic for Guyana, but Independence as a member of the British Commonwealth of Nations, with allegiance to the Queen."[31] When the National Assembly voted forty-six to two in favor of the republic resolution, the United Force provided the only opposition tallies.

Burnham, in his speech to the National Assembly in support of conversion to republic status, asserted that the change was necessitated not by any juridical limitations which the monarchy placed upon Guyana's autonomy, but essentially by psychological considerations. He noted that while it was accepted that the Queen exercised no executive powers in Guyana, "a natural fulfilment of our history should be the cutting of even formal ties" with the monarch. "Moving to the status of a republic represents," he asserted, "a further step in the direction of self-reliance and self-confidence."[32]

Burnham made it clear, however, that Guyana would not move from the symbolism of the queen to a symbolic (or historical) vacuum. He proposed Cuffy, the leader of the 1763 slave revolt in Berbice, as national hero, asserting:

> It is the contention of the party in government that the establishment of the Republic of Guyana should coincide with the celebration and/or anniversary of an event of peculiar Guyanese significance. When we were younger we remember being told about Henry V attacking at Agincourt and saying something about England and St. George. That was part of our education. Our own history was neglected, if not vilified. In fact, some of those who instructed us made a point, sometimes subtly, sometimes clumsily, of establishing to us that we had no history.
>
> A country without its own history, without its own heroes, without its own legends, I contend, would find it difficult to survive. There will be nothing to look to, nothing to admire, nothing to write or sing about. Looking over our historical landscape we came upon what is undeniably a most significant event, the slave rebellion, as it is called by some, the slave revolution, as it was called by

others, which started on the 23 February 1763, at Magdalenenberg in Berbice.

I may observe, *en passant,* that Berbice has given us not only our leader of the opposition, but also our national hero. . . .

It was decided to propose that Cuffy become our national hero and that the 207th anniversary of the revolution which he led should coincide with the date on which Guyana becomes a republic. We do not envy the British their St. George. We will not beatify Cuffy, but at least we can respect him, respect the statemanship and insight which he showed when he led the revolution.[33]

Canada, after Great Britain and the United States, has had the closest ties with Guyana of any western-group nation. Under the Canadian-West Indian Trade Agreement of 1925 a system of preferences was established. Further, the acquisition by the Aluminum Company of Canada of Aluminum Company of American bauxite mining holdings in Guyana, in the 1920's, assured Canada's interest in Guyanese affairs. In 1958 Canada embarked on an aid program in relation to the Commonwealth Caribbean. It has provided assistance to Guyana in a number of areas, particularly in the field of education.[34]

In regard to Canadian presence in the Commonwealth Caribbean region, D.A.G. Waddell, after commenting on United Kingdom ties, stated that "Commonwealth links have also been fostered with Canada, as a more acceptable trading partner and source of aid than either the mother country or the United States, which is suspected of both racism and neo-imperialism."[35]

The Canadian image in the Commonwealth Caribbean was somewhat impaired, however, as a result of the Sir George Williams University affair. In April 1968 six West Indian students at the Montreal-based university had accused a biology professor of discriminating against them in grading. Eventually a committee was established to look into the charges, but, when it met in January 1969, black students refused to participate because they considered the committee to be improperly constituted. The computer center of the University was then occupied for two weeks and, when police sought to gain control, damage estimated at between two and five million dollars occurred. Some ninety persons were arrested, among them a number of West Indians, including Cheddi Jagan, Jr., son of Guyana's Opposition Leader, and another Guyanese student, Maurice Barrow. As legal proceedings continued over the months, the affair became a *cause celebre* throughout the West Indies. Protests ensued in Guyana and throughout the region, in Trinidad contributing to the development of the "black power" revolution which reached its climax with an army mutiny in April 1970.[36]

A transition in Guyana's relations with Canada and other western nations came about through nationalization of the Aluminum Company of Canada's Demerara Bauxite Company (known locally as Demba) in 1971. Burnham, addressing his party's annual conference in April 1971, referred to Demba's broad western ties through its parent company. He argued that a multinational such as Alcan would not "integrate" its operations in Guyana (meaning utilization of Guyanese materials whenever possible in all aspects of bauxite processing, the local smelting of bauxite into aluminum and the local use of aluminum so created in fabricating products) because:

> in the first place it is not interested in Guyana's economy or economic development, and in the second place it may actually find it more *profitable to itself* to create the linkages in other parts of the world, preferably of course Europe and North America. It must be remembered that Alcan is North American and has subsidiaries and associates all over the world. It heads an empire in which insignificant specks like Guyana do not matter save as a source of valuable raw material.[37]

Aluminum Company of Canada literature has referred to Demba, prior to its nationalization in 1971, as the "oldest and largest bauxite producing unit in the Alcan group."[38] Originally a subsidiary of the Aluminum Company of America, Demba came under Alcan control after U.S. Government anti-trust action in 1927.[39] However, according to testimony before a Canadian Senate Committee in 1969 by Alcan president Nathaniel Davis, while the majority of the company's stockholders are located in Canada, the majority of its shares are held in the United States.[40] In addition to being substantially larger in scope than the other Guyana-based bauxite operation (that of Reynolds Metals Company)[41] as well as geographically more proximate to Georgetown, Demba activities had acquired a reputation for racial discrimination.[42] Thus, it was not surprising that the Alcan holdings rather than Reynolds' should have been the initial target for government participation in ownership and, with the break-down of negotiations to that end, outright nationalization.[43]

Under terms eventually agreed upon between Alcan and the Guyana government, the government is paying Alcan $53 million (U.S.) "over no more than twenty years with interest at six per cent (6%) subject to withholding tax."[44]

Nationalization of holdings in Guyana of the U.S.-based Reynolds Metals Company in 1974 and of the United Kingdom-based Booker McConnell Ltd. in 1976 have been referred to in the introductory chapter.

Guyana's ties with the nonaligned group of nations were strengthened before any marked changes occurred in her essentially distant linkages with communist countries. In September 1969, S. S. Ramphal, then heading

Guyana's delegation to the 24th Session of the United Nations General Assembly, was invited to participate in the meeting of foreign ministers of nonaligned countries at UN Headquarters. The foreign ministers arranged for a meeting in Dar es Salaam, Tanzania, the following April, apparently to finalize arrangements for the next heads of state conference of the group. At the Dar es Salaam meeting, with Guyana represented by P.S. Thompson and H.O. Jack (Thompson was then Guyana's permanent resentative at the United Nations, Jack a minister without portfolio), the summit conference was scheduled for September 1970 and Lusaka, Zambia, designated as its site. A sixteen member standing committee was elected to assist in planning for the meeting, with Guyana the only western hemisphere nation in this group. Thompson represented Guyana at meetings of the standing committee in New Delhi that June and in Lusaka in July. Thus, the stage was set for Guyana's full participation at the Lusaka summit.[45]

The Lusaka conference was critical in the nonaligned movement since it set the stage for efforts to further economic and social development by greater reliance on mutual cooperation among third world nations rather than more passive dependence on the beneficence of the developed nations. The participating governments decided "to contribute to each other's economic and social progress by an effective utilisation of the complimentarities between their respective resources and requirements" and to "co-ordinate and intensify programmes of co-operation at bilateral, regional and inter-regional levels to combine needs and resources of developing countries for furthering one another's production programmes and projects."[46]

As previously noted, Guyana was the only western hemisphere nation at the Lusaka conference represented by its political leader. Trinidad and Tobago and Cuba participated, represented by their foreign ministers, and Jamaica by its attorney general. Argentina, Barbados, Bolivia, Brazil, Chile, and Venezuela had observer status. A total of fifty-three nations participated, with twelve additional nations as observers.[47]

Guyana itself became the host for the next major nonaligned meeting. At the Conference of Foreign Ministers of Non-Aligned Countries, which met in Georgetown from August 8 to 12, 1972, sixty nations participated and eleven attended as observers. Trinidad and Tobago, Cuba, and Jamaica, along with Guyana the only western hemisphere participants at Lusaka, were joined by Chile. Argentina, Barbados, Bolivia, Brazil, and Venezuela continued in observer status, with Colombia, Ecuador, Mexico, Peru and Uruguay joining them.[48]

The major achievement of the Georgetown conference was adoption of an "Action Programme for Economic Co-Operation Among Non-Aligned Countries" which was designed to implement the Lusaka initiative toward greater cohesiveness within the group to achieve development goals. The Action Programme specified a wide range of areas, including trade, transportation, tourism, joint ventures, education, transfer of technology, and fiscal matters in which cooperation was to be enhanced. It called for "immediate action to establish or strengthen producers' associations and joint marketing arrangements in primary commodities such as copper, bauxite, tea, jute, petroleum, oil, seeds, cocoa, bananas and other commodities that may from time to time be identified.[49] Especially relevant for Guyana, in view of nationalization of the Demerara Bauxite Company in 1971 and (as matters developed) further moves in nationalization thereafter, was a portion of the Action Programme declaring that:

> Non-Aligned Countries emphatically affirm that the complete exercise of permanent sovereignty over their natural resources and the direct control of strategic economic activities, including the instruments of exploitation of such resources, in their countries, are vital to economic independence. Non-Aligned Countries therefore agree to grant their unstinting support to other developing countries which are struggling for the full and effective control of their natural resources and those strategic economic activities under foreign control. Moreover, the Non-Aligned Countries acknowledge that full control of their natural resources is a pre-requisite for effective economic co-operation among developing countries.[50]

Following the Georgetown meeting, the steering committee of the non-aligned group met in New York in December 1972 and designated Guyana as one of four nations responsible for coordinating the development of concrete plans for implementing the Action Programme. Guyana was entrusted with work pertaining to trade, industry, and transport among the nonaligned and other developing countries; Yugoslavia, in cooperation with Algeria, with technology, know-how, and technical assistance; and India, in cooperation with Indonesia, with financial and monetary cooperation for economic development.[51] Guyanese experts, working in collaboration with the Commonwealth Caribbean Regional Secretariat, and the Economic Commission for Latin America; with the assistance of experts from the Economic Commission for Africa and for Asia and the Far East and the U.N. Economic and Social Office in Beirut (handling Middle East matters), as well as of a variety of other U.N. agencies, including UNCTAD, and drawing on academicians in the Commonwealth Caribbean region, completed an extensive and detailed report in time for the nonaligned heads of state meeting held in Algiers, September 1973.[52]

Guyana's active participation in the non-aligned movement continued, with

Burnham flying from Georgetown to the September 1973 Algiers conference with Fidel Castro and Michael Manley, Prime Minister of Jamaica, in Castro's plane.

At the September 1973 heads of state meeting a statement entitled "Action Programme for Economic Co-operation" was adopted which embraced the principles developed at the Georgetown foreign ministers conference. The Georgetown conference was referred to, along with those at Belgrade, Cairo, and Lusaka, as steps in the "transition from passive submission of claims to the affirmation of the developing countries' determination to rely first and foremost on their own resources, individually and collectively, to take over the defence of their fundamental interests and to organize their development by and for themselves."[53] The report prepared by Guyana for the heads of state conference was singled out for special commendation, with the conferees declaring that they "welcomed the concrete work carried out by the co-ordinators, particularly in the field of trade, industry and transport."[54]

As Jagan had noted in commenting upon the distribution of invitations to the 1966 independence celebrations, under the coalition government official relations between Guyana and communist nations were minimal. Diplomatic relations with the U.S.S.R. were finally established in December 1970 by an exchange of notes between the Soviet Ambassador in London and Guyana's High Commissioner to Britain, with the Soviet Ambassador in Brazil named non-resident ambassador to Guyana and Guyana's High Commissioner in London named non-resident ambassador to the U.S.S.R.[55]

After the announcement of ties with the Soviet Union, which the People's Progressive Party had been pressing over the years, the PPP stressed the importance of close relations with the People's Republic of China. Noting that Burnham had recently stated in the National Assembly that "the performance of the Chinese in East Africa is, I admit, good," the PPP newspaper, *Mirror*, asked, "Why not diplomatic ties with the Chinese also?" and urged the PNC government "to start negotiations now to establish the closest possible ties with China."[56] In August 1971 a trade mission from the People's Republic visited Guyana and in November of that year a Guyanese trade delegation visited China, signing an agreement between the two countries. This resulted in establishment in March 1972 of a Chinese trade mission in Georgetown. Diplomatic relations between the countries followed in June of that year, at which point the Chinese trade mission was elevated to embassy status. In July 1973 David Singh, the Guyanese trade minister who had signed the November 1971 trade agreement in Peking, was named Guyana's first ambassador to China.[57]

In March 1975 Burnham became the first Commonwealth Caribbean head of government to visit China. While there, an agreement was signed providing for an interest-free loan of about $22 million (G), similar to a $52 million loan made by China to Guyana in 1972. Trade ties have included Chinese purchase of bauxite, sugar and timber, with Guyana reported to be purchasing "a wide variety of commodities."[58] With Chinese assistance, a claybrick factory with a capacity of 10 million bricks a year was completed as were a textile factory and a 200 bed hospital.[59]

Relations with Cuba have also expanded rapidly in the past few years. Guyana, jointly with Barbados, Jamaica, Trinidad and Tobago, announced in December 1972 establishment of diplomatic relations with Havana. The following July an agreement was signed between Guyana and Cuba for air services linking the countries, with flights beginning in October 1973. In August of that year Premier Fidel Castro visited Guyana, Prime Minister Burnham reciprocating by travelling to Havana in April 1975. During Burnham's visit, Castro paid tribute to his leadership regarding establishment of Cuban diplomatic ties by the Commonwealth Caribbean states.[60] Cuban representatives were present at both the People's Progressive Party twenty-fifth anniversary conference and the first biennial congress of the People's National Congress, both held in August 1975.[61] Since then, the two nations have exchanged resident ambassadors and have expanded already existent trade and aid ties.[62]

Ties with Eastern European countries have also been substantially increased in recent years. In November 1973 a Czechoslovakian team visited Guyana to discuss purchasing bauxite and supplying technical expertise regarding establishment of an aluminum smelter.[63] Formal diplomatic relations between Prague and Georgetown were not, however, entered into until just prior to the tenth anniversary of Guyana's independence.[64] In March 1974 a longterm trade agreement was signed with the German Democratic Republic under which the GDR was to purchase substantial quantities (over 150,000 tons annually) of bauxite and alumina. Guyana was to purchase factories, machinery, electrical products and pharmaceutical commodities.[65] Poland has apparently, along with Cuba and Peru, provided assistance in support of Guyana government fishing industry operations.[66] Yugoslavian involvement in planning the huge Upper Mazaruni hydro-electric project was mentioned in a previous chapter.

Guyana and the U.S.S.R. did not agree until February 1976 to a resident Soviet ambassador in Georgetown. The two countries had several years previously entered into a technical assistance agreement, but it apparently remained largely unimplemented until in 1976 four Guyanese took up studies in the Soviet Union, three in engineering, one in medicine.[67] The Soviet Union had, however, previously become a customer of Guyana's nationalized bauxite industry, as had China and Hungary.

Near the end of the post-independence decade, relations between Guyana and the United States, as well as with Brazil, and apparently to a lesser degree

Venezuela, became strained. Presumably "critical support" from Jagan and the PPP for the Burnham government, increasingly friendly ties with communist governments and continued moves toward national ownership of resources formerly in foreign hands were regarded, especially in the eyes of the Ford administration in Washington, as undesirable trends. In conjunction with these developments, Burnham's refusal in early 1976 to rule out use of Guyana's facilities for support of Cuban troop movements to Angola was doubtless especially unwelcome. In September 1975, not long after the PPP's critical support statement, the Brazilian daily *O Estada de Sao Paolo* had published reports alleging maltreatment of Guyana's Amerindian population. Subsequently, according to Guyana's foreign minister, the paper "misrepresented" Guyana's relations with Cuba.[68] Further, the Venezuelan weekly *Resumen* claimed on March 1, 1976 that 2,000 Cuban and Chinese troops were running four paramilitary training camps in Guyana, using Soviet and East German equipment.[69] Perhaps fearing the nation was or would be the target for external support in bringing down the government, as in the case of Chile (1973), Burnham and other Guyanese officials, supported by Jagan, charged that a destabilization campaign was underway.

Speaking at ceremonies commemorating the sixth anniversary of conversion to republic status in February 1976, Burnham stated that Guyana's nonaligned policy meant friendship with all who would be friendly with the country, declaring that the government would not permit its territory to be used as a base hostile to any hemispheric state. However, he asserted that the country was now subjected to "the most vicious attacks and prevarications by certain elements in other countries and certain sections of the foreign media " He referred to "some hawks" who "are bent on discrediting Guyana and laying the basis for intervention and/or destabilisation."[70]

The *Caribbean Monthly Bulletin* noted that official sources in Guyana had "revealed on April 26 (1976) that there is a tense situation developing on Guyana's border with Brazil, Venezuela and Surinam." Reports of a Brazilian troop buildup and of Venezuela troop reinforcements in border areas as well as of Surinam personnel in a disputed area were referred to. Home Minister Vibert Mingo was quoted as advising, in an address to policemen at a hinterland outpost:

> We have not reached the stage of war but we are not far from it. It means therefore that you have got to be a little more vigilant. Keep your ears to the ground and report every bit of information to your superiors so that it can be processed as soon as possible.[71]

Eventually, however, the tensions subsided and more friendly relations appeared to prevail not only with Guyana's neighbors, but (following installation of the Carter administration in January 1977) with the United States.[72]

In surveying the transitions in Guyana's external linkages during the first ten years of independence, one can note first that little movement was possible during the coalition with the United Force Party (in effect until late 1968), and probably little could be anticipated until the border disputes had been, at least on an interim basis, resolved [73] With the coalition ended and the territorial claims "shelved," the Burnham government was in a position to both deal with foreign ownership of the nation's resources and to begin a shifting of international relationships. Firm ties with Cuba and the U.S.S.R. were apparently not possible, given the People's Progressive Party's long-standing friendships with these nations, while the PPP remained adamantly critical of the PNC government. This obstacle was removed, however, with the "critical support" accorded the PNC government by the PPP in August 1975.

Just how completely "nonaligned" Guyana was as of May 1976 is a matter of controversy. In an interview published on the tenth independence anniversary, Foreign Minister Fred Wills stated that "Guyana is non-aligned and is charting a course which seeks to avoid bloc entanglements" and also to insure a transition "from the state of colonial disadvantages to the just society implicit in our philosophy towards socialism "[74]

Clive Thomas, on the other hand, asserted at about the same time that "the harsh fact is that despite the nationalizations, etc. the overwhelming bulk of our trade, investment, foreign debt, training and cultural ties is still with the capitalist and imperialist countries."[75] Two years earlier somewhat the same position had been taken by Basil Ince who, while finding Guyana closer to nonalignment than Jamaica, Barbados and Trinidad and Tobago, concluded that a pragmatic awareness of the "hegemonic shadow of the United States" has resulted "in a situation in which Guyana's foreign policy, despite her profession of neutralism and non-alignment, has tended to be more pro-western than neutral."[76]

Undoubtedly, further time must pass before any definitive assessment of Guyana's long-run alignments can be made. In the meantime, it seems at the least apparent that meaningful transition has taken place and that in a world in which "nonalignment" is seldom achieved in a mathematically pure sense, Guyana has made dramatic strides in that direction.

Chapter 6

Toward Nondependent Development

When Guyana became independent in 1966 it was subject to external dependency for major resource components and in regard to key aspects of technology. The dependency linkages were principally to its primary metropolitan powers, Great Britain, the United States and Canada. William Demas had underscored the subordinate position of Commonwealth Caribbean polities in resource relationships when he asserted in 1965 that

> the economies are very dependent, not only structurally in the sense that there is a high ratio of foreign trade to Gross Domestic Product, but also in that there is great reliance on foreign private capital inflows and foreign aid, there is little financial and monetary autonomy, and there are still important gaps in the domestic financial structure. Foreign decision-making is all-pervasive and touches many parts of economic and financial life.[1]

With specific reference to Guyana, Ved Duggal pointed out several years after independence.

> Total domestic capital formation is financed heavily by foreign resources. Foreign banks in Guyana also finance consumer credit and thus siphon off household savings. . . . All this has resulted in the dependence of the economy on foreign capital. Historically, foreign capital has owned the most profitable sectors of production, such as sugar and bauxite. It has also dominated the foreign and wholesale trade, banking, insurance and shipping.[2]

Continuation of reliance on external resources was a basic assumption of Guyana's first independence-period development plan. This plan, evolved by a working party headed by W. Arthur Lewis, the St. Lucian-born economist, and involving specialists from Guyana, Britain, Canada, the United States, and the United Nations,[3] called for capital expenditures by the Government over the seven-year period totaling approximately $295 million Guyanese.[4] Of this sum, it was projected that $245 million, or some 83%, would come from external sources ($100 million in grants, $100 million in "soft" loans at 5% interest, and $45 million in "hard" loans at 11% interest), with the balance of $50 million from internal borrowings.[5] The quarter from which such external funds would be sought was strongly hinted at by Prime Minister Burnham in his preface to the plan when he stated that "Placed as we are geographically as a small nation that has contributed to the economic progress of the old world, we shall be anxious to employ their finance, technology and experience for our national good."[6] Burnham did add that "We welcome from the rest of the world aid that can be made to fit in with the self determined national purpose."[7] However, as noted in the preceding chapter, while there had been offers of assistance from eastern or communist countries in the years from 1960 to 1964, there was no aid relationship with this sector during the post-independence period until after the establishment of economic ties with the People's Republic of China in 1971.

The quantum of external grants and loans for government use projected in the 1966-72 plan was not received. The total amount received for the period covered by the plan was slightly under $160 million (Guyanese), or almost $85 million short of the plan's projection of $245 million. Grants totaled slightly under $34 million, short by approximately $66 million, and loans totaled just under $126 million, short by approximately $19 million. As is indicated by these figures, fulfillment of plan goals was more nearly achieved in regard to loans than grants.[8]

In view of the shortage of resources to fulfill the projections, and for a variety of other reasons, the 1966-72 plan was revised periodically and eventually scrapped, apparently in 1970. A new plan, covering the five years from 1972 through 1976 but not completed or published until 1973, provided for a much greater proportion of internally-generated capital funding (in relation to external capital) than the defunct plan. The plan called for a total of $1151 million in gross domestic fixed investment over the five-year period and envisaged $748 million (65% of the total) coming from domestic savings against $413 million (35% of the total) from external sources.[9]

The 1966-72 plan had placed considerable emphasis on stimulation and encouragement of private investment in the Guyanese economy, including investment from foreign sources. The plan listed concessions offered to investors, including a tax holiday for five years from commencement of production, subsidization of industrial sites, accelerated write-off of building, machinery, and equipment costs, and absence of restriction of repatriation of profits or of capital gains.[10] The plan's presentation also underscores, "As further evidence of this Government's willingness to encourage foreign investors," an agreement entered into with the United States government guaranteeing investments in Guyana by Americans, asserting that "Guyana thus become part of that area in which the U.S. Government feels that its nationals can invest with confidence."[11] In view of the emphasis on private foreign capital attracted through such incentives and guarantees, the 1966-72 plan and similar approaches to economic development in other Commonwealth Caribbean polities have often been referred to as based upon the Puerto Rican, or "industrialization by invitation," model.[12]

The 1966-72 plan did not set out detailed targets for private investment, including the foreign component thereof, stating that "there is little accurate information about the country's real resources" and that for "detailed targets to be useful, they must be firmly based."[13] However, the program presentation did assert that "While the total saving and investment steadily rise over the plan period, the proportion represented by private investment (under 50% in 1966) will rise by the end of the period," noting that "This reflects the large increases in investment and output that are expected from the private sector."[14]

The 1972-76 development plan substantially de-emphasized the role of private foreign investment. Policy statements contained in the program presentation such as "When natural resources of the nation are to be exploited in partnership with non-nationals, the State reserves the right to seek majority ownership and control or to share that control with Co-operatives alone to be the major partner"[15] replace the generally unqualified welcome for foreign investment contained in the 1966-72 plan. Investment incentives were to be continued, although the plan's language was not as explicit with regard to the terms of such incentives as was the 1966-72 plan.[16]

The 1972-76 development plan places great emphasis upon national self-sufficiency, especially in regard to food, clothing, and housing. The plan presentation, after stating in a chapter which seeks to provide a perspective for understanding plan goals that "Guyana must be self-reliant.... Guyana must itself produce the basic requirement of its people, and must itself determine the pace and direction of its social and economic development,"[17] declares that

> it has been decided that the main thrust of development during the plan period should be directed towards Feeding, Clothing and Housing the nation. These objectives have been chosen for several reasons. First, it is considered to be the duty of the Government of Guyana to make available to the nationals of Guyana the means of acquiring the basic necessities of life. Secondly, the pursuit of the objectives of feeding, clothing and housing ourselves would result in the creation of a considerable number of employment opportunities, through the backward and forward linkages which will be provided. Thirdly, feeding, clothing and housing ourselves would lead to a significant expansion of the economy. And fourthly, these developments, spread as they must be, in the hinterland, in the rural

areas and in the cities, and embracing as they do the forestry, agricultural, manufacturing, building, mining and service sectors, would lead to a more equitable spatial and functional distribution of economic activity.[18]

With specific regard to food, the plan, in a chapter devoted to agriculture, speaks of "fulfillment of the national goal of feeding the Nation by 1976 with food of high nutritive content."[19] The presentation also notes the impact of "imported attitudes" on patterns of production and consumption, asserting:

> There is in Guyana a range of locally produced foodstuffs which must be the envy of gourmets the world over. Nevertheless, there has been a tendency in the country to consume foods which we were forced to import in the past because of our dependence then on external cultures and because of "passive" foreign trade policies. Similarly, our tastes and contentions with regard to clothing have been largely imported and in conflict with our own environment. In recent years ["buy local" has been a governmentally encouraged motto since independence in 1966], this propensity to prefer non-Guyanese commodities and fashions has changed to some degree. However, there is still considerable room for improvement.[20]

The plan points toward increasing self-reliance in a variety of sectors, stating:

> Although the main plan in the development programme is the achievement of self-sufficiency in food, clothing and houses, other areas of development will not be neglected. There will also be expansion in such sectors as mining and quarrying (not directly associated with the self-sufficiency programme), engineering, transport and communications. In these sectors, efforts will be concentrated on the utilization of our natural resources, on the provision of surpluses for export and on the establishment and expansion of those activities which are export-oriented.[21]

A goal of enhancing trading ties with "miscellaneous Non-European/Non-American countries," apparently a euphemistic reference to communist nations, is indicated in the 1972-76 development plan. Noting that United Kingdom export prices had increased by about 25% between 1963 and 1971, the plan presentation points out that prices had a much slower increase from "the miscellaneous Non-European/Non-American countries." After underscoring a drop in the proportion of the value of imports from these "miscellaneous Non-European/Non-American countries" in the 1963-71 period, the presentation states that "It is here that the Government's foreign trade policy and the operations of the External Trade Bureau [established in July 1970 with special responsibilities in regard to imports from communist nations] are expected to change such structural imbalances in our external payments."[22]

Under a heading "Greater CARIFTA and Third World Trade," the 1972-1976 plan presentation states that

> In response to the greater demand for local production, such surpluses as will be produced will seek CARIFTA markets, other markets in our neighboring territories, and overseas markets further away. Similarly, the machinery and equipment requirements for our import replacement programme will be increasingly met from those sources in which the terms and conditions are favorable and for which the machinery and equipment that are obtainable are more suited to our technological standards and to our environmental conditions. Trade with the Third World in general, and with our CARIFTA partners in particular, will be encouraged.[23]

In regard to economic ties with other developing nations, Forbes Burnham had stated in the National Assembly debate on foreign policy in March 1967 that such countries could, "in spite of their limited resources, develop not only formal political links but trade and economic links, and come together for their mutual benefit and protection.[24] Foreshadowing the later development of raw material producers' association, including the International Bauxite Associations, he asserted that "This can be done especially in cases where they are the sole producers of certain important commodities, goods and or minerals."[25]

Ptolemy Reid, speaking as finance minister, emphasized trade and other economic relations with developing nations when he presented the 1971 budget in the National Assembly in the first budget submission since Guyana's participation at the Lusaka conference of nonaligned countries. The conference, he asserted,

> spot-lighted the need for more determined efforts on the part of developing nations to forge closer trade and other economic links among themselves, the importance of the policy of ownership and control of their own resources, and the need, in the language of the Lusaka Declaration,

> "to employ international machinery to bring about the rapid transformation of the world economic system particularly in the field of trade, finance and technology so that economic domination yields to economic co-operation and economic strength is used for the benefit of the world community; to view the development

process in a global context and to adopt a programme of
international action for utilization of world resources in men and
materials, science and technology benefiting developed and
developing nations alike."[26]

In his remarks at the April 1974 special session of the U.N. General
Assembly, S.S. Ramphal pointed to the relatively meager trade and other
economic relationships among developing countries but emphasized efforts to
enhance such ties:

> Through the long imperial centuries the links which had once bound
> so many of the peoples of the southern zone of the world were
> broken as a matter of deliberate policy. It was the vocation of
> "Bandung", and of the non-aligned movement which has univers-
> alized the objectives of that Conference, to rebuild those links, and
> to do so first of all at the political level.
>
> In the area of economic activity the pattern unhappily is still one
> of fragmentation with the flow of goods and transport and
> techniques following the imperial routes. But here, too, change is
> under way; and arising out of the decisions of the non-aligned
> movement to embark on an action programme of economic co-
> operation among developing States, measures of co-operation and
> collective self-reliance which are now ripe for implementation in
> such areas as the development of trade, industry and transport, the
> transfer of technology and joint action in the field of monetary
> issues, represent a major step towards removing the developing
> States from their present peripheral position in the international
> economy and making for a more equitable division of labour.[27]

In his presentation of the 1969 budget, Reid had pointed to problems posed
by external grants and loans and the resultant need for increased reliance on
domestic sources for the nation's development:

> .... external assistance usually comes with specific terms. The
> funds are tied to the provision of local counterpart finance, and, in
> most cases, they are provided by the aid-donor for specific projects.
> While we certainly appreciate receiving this assistance from friendly
> foreign Governments, and International agencies, it must be clear
> that financing the development Budget from external loan funds
> introduces certain unfortunate rigidities into the development
> programme that is implemented. If, therefore, there is to be the
> flexibility that is desirable for implementation of its programme,
> more and more funds must come from domestic sources. The rate

of saving must be increased and more of these funds must be made available to the Government for development purposes.[28]

More recently, in the speech delivered in connection with unveiling the 1974 budget, a new minister of finance, Frank Hope, cited interest rates in world money markets for short and medium term loans in excess of 13% and asserted that in view of the high cost of foreign borrowing it was "of utmost importance that Guyanese should rely more on domestic savings for the financing of development works."[29]

At the PNC annual meeting in May 1973, Burnham, in commenting on the draft 1972-76 development plan, which he noted "premises the expenditure and/or deployment of well over one thousand million dollars of resources," stated:

> The point may be made that this represents the largest programme ever contemplated over a similar period in the history of Guyana. To my mind, however, that is not a point of great significance. What is much more important is that sixty-five per cent of the expenditure is proposed to be provided from our own internal resources directly. This is based on the confidence that it is within our nation's capability, and a practical projection of our national philosophy of self-reliance.
>
> To the conservative and orthodox this is a leviathan undertaking for a nation of three quarter million souls; but so was independence, and so was the nationalisation of the Alcan subsidiary, Demba.[30]

Regarding dependence in terms of technology, the comments of J.J. Villamil, H. Ortiz and E.R. Gutierrez provide a useful framework of reference:

> It is obvious that technology transfers are embodied in capital flows ... [and] these transfers involve an exporter and an importer. Underdeveloped countries are for the most part importers. In effect, one can use the phrase technological dependence to describe the condition of most underdeveloped countries.
>
> Political ties are an influence in the sense that they determine the trading partners of countries. . . . Even so, there is much that dependent countries can do with respect to augmenting their control over technology transfers and their effects. . . . Schumacher has placed great emphasis on the development of what he terms "intermediate technology" as an answer to this problem [31]

Guyana's 1966-72 development plan did not present proposals for dealing with technological dependence and problems associated with the application of unsuitable techniques. However, in the 1972-76 program, as well as in statements by Prime Minister Burnham following conversion to republic status, considerable emphasis is placed upon the importance of utilizing technologies which are appropriate in the Guyanese context and for Guyanese involvement and decision-making in questions pertaining to application, adaptation, and innovation of technology. Likewise, in the declarations of the nonaligned movement, including those resulting from the 1972 Georgetown foreign ministers conference, attention is given to the problems associated with technological dependence and proposals are made for greater cooperation among the nonaligned or developing nations in decreasing such dependence.

The 1972-76 development plan, in discussing the goal of national self-reliance, states that "it means that Guyanese nationals must possess the skills and expertise that are necessary to run and manage a modern State effectively, that they must believe that they are capable of doing so." The plan further declares that "Guyanese must control technological changes within their society, and must ensure that such changes fulfil social as well as economic objectives."[32] The plan is replete with statements pertaining to the application, misapplication and nonapplication of technology in the Guyanese context. It lists, among undesirable features which foreign enterprises will have to discard if they are to contribute more fully to the nation's development, "inappropriate technology";[33] it asserts that majority participation by the government or cooperatives in key sectors is the best way of ensuring "that technological know-how is transmitted to and developed within the Guyanese economy";[34] in discussing incentives for private investment it states that "Special concessions will be provided for industries which increase the level of their local value added, especially when such increases are associated with technology that is labour oriented."[35] With specific reference to the bauxite sector, it states that "because it was wholly owned and controlled by foreign investors, the industry, during its fifty years of operation under foreign ownership, was isolated from the rest of the economy and offered no stimulus to the development of technological, marketing and entrepreneurial expertise in other sectors, and to the development of other industries by backward and forward linkages."[36] In a chapter titled "Plan Implementation and Institutional Changes," it asserts that "The recently established National Research and Scientific Council will give the necessary direction in a wide field of research, particularly with respect to the greater utilisation of our natural resources, the adaptation of relevant technologies and the most pressing social and economic problems."[37]

At the PNC's annual conference in April 1971, Burnham spoke with scorn of growth without meaningful development resulting from misapplication of technology imported from Europe and North America:

So often in countries like ours, development is approached with a
complex that we are too poor to do it. Projects are conceived in
terms of frightening millions representing all foreign inputs of goods,
services and skills. In addition, a technology frequently irrelevant
and socially expensive is employed—the capital intensive technology.
People do not seem to understand that the capital intensive
technology to be found in Europe and North America came after, in
most cases, a shortage of labour. We, in Guyana, with a surplus of
labour, consider it the epitome of sophistication and development to
be using machines which we do not understand, cannot construct
and can hardly move. In the context of a surplus of labour, high-
cost sophisticated labour-saving machines are used, giving employment to only a few. Further, local materials are often ignored and
their substitutes imported.

Then, when we do these things, importing everything, using an
irrelevant technology which creates the minimum number of jobs,
we are told by the conventional economists that we are witnessing
growth. Then we witness growth, sometimes a most illusory concept,
and no real development. Poverty and unemployment continue to
stalk the land. Social instability supervenes, disillusionment follows
and anarchy and chaos threaten.[38]

Addressing the PNC annual meeting in May 1973, with the goals of
national self-sufficiency in food, clothing, and housing set out in the 1972-76
development plan in mind, Burnham spoke in concrete terms with regard to
utilization of relevant technology:

It has been estimated that the exercise of clothing ourselves will
provide directly, in the early stages, about two thousand new jobs or
employment opportunities.

The site for the textile mill has been identified and experiments in
cotton growing have so far been most favourable and reassuring.
Guyana, as some of us may know, in the late 19th and the early
years of the 20th century, was the world's number two producer of
raw cotton. But will we find when cotton is grown, Guyanese
clamouring for large, sophisticated machines to do the picking?

We have, as a people, been adversely affected by the developed
countries of North America and Europe in at least one respect.
These countries have had to mechanise and introduce some of the
most complicated and sophisticated machines and equipment

because of their own conditions and circumstances, one of which is a relative shortage of labour.

In any case, they manufacture the machines utilised within their own borders and economies. We do not manufacture these and therefore have to purchase them with our slender foreign resources. Further, far from having a labour shortages, we have at our present stage of development, a surplus of this factor of production.

Whenever, therefore, we use a machine to do what men or women can do, we are contributing to continued unemployment and individual and national poverty. Technology must be relevant to prevailing circumstances, otherwise it can be a millstone around our neck. We here, we PNC members, must understand this simple fact and by example and precept bring about the necessary attitudinal readjustment in Guyana.[39]

As to cooperation among developing nations in achieving relevant technological progress and in sharing techniques, the "Declaration on Non-Alignment and Economic Progress" adopted at the Lusaka Conference of nonaligned nations in September 1970 called for the organization of "means and measures to share one another's experience in the application of science and technology to processes of economic and social development" and for the devising of "programmes for adoption [adaptation?] of technology to the special needs of countries in different stages of development, and to provide for its widest possible diffusion to developing countries and for the conservation of their technical skills and personnel in consonance with their needs and conditions."[40]

Likewise, the "Action Programme for Economic Cooperation" adopted at the Georgetown conference of foreign ministers of nonaligned countries in August 1972, in a section entitled "Co-operation in the Field of Research, Science and Technology Including the Transfer of Technology and Technological Know-how," declared that nonaligned countries should "encourage the sharing of techniques and cross-fertilisation of ideas among their experts in specific fields," "encourage the exchange of information of new achievements in the field of technology and patterns on a preferential or a reciprocal basis," "establish joint institutes for scientific research at major industrial enterprises among them, for the purpose of research and the training of cadres geared to the special problems of developing countries," and "devise programmes to adapt technology to the production structures, economic and social conditions (including the unemployment situation) and the natural resource endowments of the Non-aligned Countries."[41]

At their September 1973 conference in Algiers, the heads of state of nonaligned nations adopted an "Economic Declaration," one portion of which recognizes "the need for developing countries to bridge the gap between them and the industrialized world in the field of technology."[42] In the "Action Programme for Economic Co-operation" also adopted at Algiers, the heads of state, in a section titled "Transfer of Technology," asserted:

> The provisions as regards the transfer of technology in the International Development Strategy [of the United Nations General Assembly] will need to be implemented without delay, and the developing countries should take a joint stand on this question in international bodies. . . . Monopolistic practices, applied by transnational corporations through market-sharing and price-fixing, should be ended and the costs of transferring technology to developing countries reduced. . . . New international legislation for the transfer of technology to the developing countries on a preferential basis should be formulated and an international code of conduct should be adopted and implemented without delay. . . . Urgent measures should be taken at both national and international levels to stop the brain-drain from developing to developed countries"[43]

The Action Programme also asserted, with regard to foreign private investment, that it should be subject to prior authorization for the purpose of insuring, among other considerations listed, that it "incorporates appropriate technology, leads to the further development of technology," and "generates employment."[44] In a section of the Action Programme headed "Co operation with Socialist Countries," the assertion is made that "Socialist countries should accord the most favourable terms for intensifying trade, economy, scientific and technical co-operation with non-aligned countries. Special action should be considered in the fields of transfer of technology and training of national personnel of developing countries."[45]

During the first half of the post independence decade, Guyana was almost entirely dependent on western sources for technical assistance in the field of agriculture and for help in locating and tapping mineral and hydro-electric resources. However, as noted in the preceding chapter, from 1971 onward there has been increasing diversification, with communist nations and to an extent other developing nations playing a role.

Efforts to enhance Guyana's own capabilities for technological innovation and development have been pursued during the post-independence period under study. The 1966-72 development plan provided for capital expenditures for a program of technical training at the University of Guyana, for equipment at the Technical Institute in Georgetown, and for establishment of a technical institute at the country's second city, New Amsterdam.[46] The 1972-76 development plan provides for further capital expenditures for technical education and notes that a higher technical diploma course in mechanical engineering and a bachelor of technology program were to start at the University of Guyana during the plan period.[47] Efforts have also been made to recruit Guyanese residing abroad who have needed skills, including, in some cases, on a short term basis.[48]

A step toward enhancing Commonwealth Caribbean regional cooperation in the fields of science and technology was taken in 1973 when delegates at the eighteenth scientific meeting of the Standing Advisory Committee for Medical Research, held in Georgetown, voted for establishment of a Commonwealth Caribbean Research Council. In addressing the conferees, Prime Minister Burnham assured his government's support, including financial backing, and stated that "In the West Indies or the Caribbean, we could never earn the name NATION, if we do not, by financing or by the setting up of institutions, provide the facilities for relevant research in the circumstances of the region."[49] Previously, in April 1970, the heads of government conference of the Commonwealth Caribbean had adopted proposals regarding the establishment of a Commonwealth Technical Assistance Programme, agreeing that it would be administered by the regional secretariat.[50] The Guyanese publication reporting this decision also noted that Guyana had already received technical assistance from various Commonwealth Caribbean territories, including Barbados, Trinidad and Tobago and Jamaica. It further noted that training had been provided in programs in Guyana to public officers from a number of Commonwealth Caribbean polities and that "on-the-spot" and practical training in fields such as geological survey, community and economic development, and the development of roads and airstrips had been provided in Dominica, Montserrat, St. Lucia and St. Vincent.[51]

As indicated here and in the previous chapter regarding global alignments, increasingly in the period from 1969 onward the Burnham government has sought to broaden resource and technology ties and to foster self-reliant development where feasible. Marked though policy shifts in this regard have been, much remains to be done if dependence on traditional metropolitan powers is to be lessened substantially.

Yet the infra-structure of change is now at least partially in place. Guyana has shown impressive capabilities for developing and fostering resource and technology-sharing relationships with other developing nations and to a lesser extent with developed communist nations. It has also shown the ability to train and utilize its own people for a self-development thrust as well as for enhancing cooperative relations with other third world countries. Thus there is ample evidence for concluding that the nation's future with regard to resources and technology is likely to involve further enhancement of internal capacity as well as increasing diversification of external linkages.

Chapter 7

Identity in Transition

Group identity within a nation-state involves a complex of factors, but among the most critical in many cases, and certainly in that of Guyana, are ethnic, social class, cultural and ideological factors. Often, these elements overlap and intertwine and this is especially true for a people emerging from colonialism. Pablo Gonzalez-Casanova has characterized the colonial situation in the following terms:

> Racism and racial segregation are essential in the colonial exploitation of some peoples by others. They influence all configurations of development in colonial cultures. They are a brake in the processes of acculturation. In the interchange and transmission of advanced techniques to the dominated population, in the occupational mobility of native workers who tend to remain in unskilled jobs, in the political and administrative mobility of the native people, racism and discrimination correlate with the psychology of colonialism.[1]

Gonzalez-Casanova's analysis is as relevant for a colonized area such as Guyana, in which the bulk of the population was brought in either through slavery or indenture, as for one in which political and economic domination were established over existing peoples. For Guyana, as long as the colonial frame of reference held sway, the highest status to which one could aspire was that of acceptance in the British empire, with whiteness next to godliness and imperial class, cultural and ideological values constituting the imposed norm.[2]

However, the colonization process was not uniform in its effects on different groups within the population. Africans were more susceptible to it than East Indians, because they, as slaves, had been stripped to a greater extent of their own cultures and as a group had been socialized in the colony for a longer period. Portuguese and "mixed" groups were far more susceptible than either, given their preferential standing by dint of "European blood" and concomitant phenotypical attributes, including skin color, facial characteristics, and texture of hair.[3] Further, under certain circumstances, colonial values could not be relied upon to assure unimpeded imperial control. This was demonstrated by the mass unrest and disturbances of the first four decades of this century, especially in the 1930's.[4] The emergence in 1950 of the People's Progressive Party, projecting an uncompromising anti-imperialist orientation, seemed to provide assurance that once independence was achieved, Guyana would not be contained within the imposed, colonial assumptions.

This assurance was undermined, however, when the People's National Congress-United Force coalition government came into office in late 1964. Not only had the coalition received British and United States (that is, broadly speaking, "European") backing in achieving power, but the United Force component amalgamated portions of the population which were among those most conducive to perpetuation of colonial society—middle class Portuguese and Chinese, as well as "mixed" or "colored." Further, while the PNC had a mass following among Africans, it too, partly as a result of a merger with the conservative United Democratic Party in 1959, represented substantial middle-class components and could hardly be regarded as a reliable base for decolonization, the socialist and anti-imperialist past of Burnham and others of its leaders notwithstanding.[5]

Thus, as independence came to Guyana, there were ample grounds for serious doubt as to whether any meaningful reorientation in ethnic, class, cultural, and ideological moorings could or would take place in the foreseeable future. The coalition government continued to be heavily dependent upon its metropolitan mentors for financial support, for training of defense and police forces, and ultimately for assistance in putting down a revolt by East Indians, should that occur. Further, with another national election to be held some time within the next nineteen months, and with no realistic prospects for cutting into Jagan's and the PPP's hold on the East Indian population, Burnham's strategy was apparently to shore up his base among the Africans, insure their continued domination of defense, police, and civil service forces, and with their support "tough out" a "non-election" in which his PNC could emerge "victorious" and coalition-free.[6] Once out of harness with the United Force, and having demonstrated the PNC's capacity for maintaining power in spite of PPP electoral strength (since elections would no longer be meaningful in a competitive sense), it would be *possible* to move toward a more indigenous assertion of Guyanese personality, with all the internal and external ramifications of such a reorientation.

However, whether such a reorientation would in fact occur depended upon many factors, not the least important of which was the self-conceptualization of Burnham and his key associates—whether they would view themselves as leaders of an ideological-ethnic faction, maintaining control by repression, or as leaders of a nation in the process of achieving more cohesive harmony. In the end, doubtless aware of the meager and ultimately disparaging standing in history which a narrow projection of their role would have insured, they opted for an attempt at cohesion, and therefore for decolonization. Their capabilities, and Guyana's potential for a more dynamic nationhood (a potential to which Cheddi and Janet Jagan, as well as other PPP leaders, had made no small contribution) asserted themselves, with consequences still being experienced within the nation, as well as in, and beyond, the Caribbean.

Two interrelated questions warrant consideration at this point: a) would it have been possible to decolonize internally without any transformation of external relations? and b) if not, what sorts of transformation of external ethnic, social class, cultural, and ideological relationships would decolonization entail?

The first question must be answered negatively since, as previously indicated, the assumptions of colonial society were external in their groundings. The referent "ideal" was European (English). The ideal had been imposed by the colonizer and perpetuated within the colony by an elite which depended on the colonizer's favor and power. Any meaningful shift would, in these circumstances, necessarily involve external relationships.

The answer to the second question is more complicated, since the options open to the nation's leaders were varied. However, in the ethnically, culturally, and ideologically plural society which Guyana epitomized at the time of independence, any choices regarding external referents would have positive or negative (or mixed) consequences in regard to internal cohesion. Thus, for instance, while the Commonwealth Caribbean region provided an alternative ethnic environment in contrast to perpetuating European (including North American) ties, its population was so overwhelmingly African (with the exception of Trinidad and Tobago, and even in that case Africans predominate over East Indians by a ratio of approximately nine to seven), that, pushed too far over too lengthy a period, close ties could easily provoke heightened polarization between Africans and East Indians in Guyana. By the same token, an ideological shift from values emanating from Great Britain and the newer metropolitan power centers (the United States and Canada) to those of the communist nations might be favorably regarded by the leadership of the PPP, and perhaps even by significant elements of that party's mass following. However, such a shift could hardly be expected to appeal to those supporters of the PNC (to say nothing of the United Force) whose position was that Cheddi Jagan must be denied power precisely because he represented a "trojan horse" in terms of such views. Thus, the choices for the PNC leadership were in fact somewhat circumscribed, lying in the direction, at least initially, of the more ethnically diverse and ideologically eclectic "third world "

Ethnic Aspects

Broadly defined, ethnic includes cultural elements. However, in dealing with ethnic identity, this work focuses upon elements involving genetically transmittable physical characteristics (sometimes referred to as "racial" characteristics). A separate cultural category is utilized with reference to those elements which operate through processes of socialization rather than through more definitively genetic processes.

In recent years there has been a trend in some circles toward perceiving a system of ethnic dualism at the world level, with European (meaning "white") populations dominating non-European populations (also referred to as "non-white," "colored," or "black"). A popularized version of this conceptualization was put forth in Ronald Segal's *The Race War,* published in 1967. In the introductory chapter of this work, Segal asserts:

> The world is dominated by the white states (including, of course, the Soviet Union) which profit from contemporary conditions and consequently resist any serious attempt at change. But contemporary conditions are, for the mass of humanity, unbearable, and it is precisely change, of the most fundamental kind, that the mass of humanity needs. To suppose that the white states will surrender their dominance without compulsion is denied alike by history and common sense. And the only compulsion that coloured people can employ lies in their own efforts.[7]

Somewhat in line with Segal's analysis, James Moss has commented that "The line between rich nations and poor and the line between white and non-white are dangerously near coinciding and the polarisation of the world into camps divided by these lines becomes increasingly serious."[8]

George Shepherd and Tilden LeMelle have expressed their perception of evolving white-nonwhite dichotomization in the following terms:

> The bond of color in opposition to actual or perceived white domination has crossed not only black national boundaries but also those of yellow and brown peoples. The Bandung Conference of 1955 of African and Asian peoples was the first explicitly called to unite "peoples of color" against white domination and oppression. Specifically using the argument of race, China was successful in keeping Russia out of the Bandung meeting making it an international conference of non-white peoples. The policies of racial discrimination in South Africa and the United Kingdom increasingly are moving Indians and other Asians to refer to themselves as

black—black symbolizing a transcendence of nationality, religion, culture and sex to combat white dominance. It would not be out of place here to mention the new alliance in the United States between young whites, brown Puerto Ricans and blacks united under the symbol of the Black Panther against white domination. The rhetoric of these groups clearly makes them a part of the world revolution of color.

History has provided and still provides much evidence of transnational white ties in support of white domination over non-white peoples. The evidence of transnational racial ties in opposition to white domination is still sketchy but increasing. But its impact has already reached South Africa where continued white dominance is sustained by the white world. If the pattern continues on both sides of the racial lines, the international system cannot but experience increased racial dysfunction and incoherence. States cannot secede from international intercourse nor can whole races any longer be isolated or controlled as under white colonialism. International racial equality will obtain or the world will be engulfed in racial war.[9]

Guyana's increasing ties with the non-European or "black" aspect of the ethnic environment in recent years have been clearly evidenced. In addition to a heightened commitment to regional and third world solidarity, as discussed in previous portions of this study, there has been a marked upswing in support of ethnic liberation movements. In February 1970, for instance, during the week of observances commemorating conversion to the Co-operative Republic, Georgetown was the site of a conference of Pan-African and black revolutionaries. The Conference had been organized by ASCRIA (the African Society for Cultural Relations with Independent Africa). Speaking at the opening of the conference, which was attended by a number of Afro-Americans as well as participants from the Caribbean, Prime Minister Burnham stated:

> To those of you who have come from the United States of America, may I say that I think I am aware of some of your problems. I hope to have an opportunity of speaking to you more informally and to learn more about these problems. I sometimes think, maybe I am wrong but I think that I am right, that you live in a hostile jungle. You live in a society which is noted for its violent suppression of your rights but calls upon you to be better than Jesus and to indulge in non-violence. We in Guyana, who have passed

through the crucible, understand some of your problems and we hope to understand them even better when you will have left.[10]

Addressing himself to a theme which had come to the fore in the black power movement in the United States, the role in the liberation process of non-members of the group seeking liberation, Burnham asserted:

> If you will forgive me, as one black man to others, I will say that the problem with our organisations in the past has been that we have not shown enough faith and confidence in ourselves, and we have allowed the representatives and agents of our enemies to come in like wood ants and destroy what we have been trying to build even before we have really started building.
>
> We must learn to have confidence in ourselves and confidence to achieve what we set out to achieve without other people taking over. It does not mean that we must not speak to them, it does not mean that we must not discuss with them, but when we do, it must always be on the basis of our organisation holding a dialogue with those outside of the organisation. I find it disgusting sometimes to see so many non-blacks, more black than the black people in black organisations. . . .
>
> We, in Guyana, have learnt by bitter experience, and I hope that we have learnt completely and fully, that cooperation or willingness to discuss with others must never mean subordination of ourselves to these "do-gooders."[11]

Placing his government on record in support of liberation, in the United States, in the Caribbean, and in Africa, Burnham declared:

> The Government and the people of Guyana recognise, that the struggle in those parts of the yet politically unemancipated countries of Africa, the struggles of the black people in the United States of America, the struggles of the people in the Caribbean to own and control their countries at the economic level, are all part of one major struggle of the black man in the world today. Some of you may not know, but Guyana is perhaps the only country in the Caribbean that has given political asylum to freedom fighters from the continent of Africa, and that is because we don't believe merely in talking.
>
> We feel deeply, and whatever contribution we can make to the emancipation, the liberation of the black man wherever he may be,

Identity in Transition 91

we are willing to make, even if it means sacrifices on our part.[12]

Burnham projected his perception of Guyana as under attack by Venezuela on an ethnic basis, stating:

> We, in Guyana, have learnt and continue to learn in the hard school. Today, as we are celebrating the birth of our Cooperative Republic, the only coloured Republic on the American Continent, the Venezuelans, and you can describe them ethnically, are out to destroy our nation and to seize our territory. It is difficult for us to escape the conclusion that it is because we are a coloured nation that they have suddenly discovered that practically the whole of our country belongs to them, the members of the "master race".[13]

Burnham went beyond verbal support for liberation when, during the Lusaka Conference of Non-Aligned Nations in September 1970, he presented to President Julius Nyerere of Tanzania a check for $50,000 (Guyanese) to support freedom fighters in Southern Africa. The presentation was made on behalf of the Government and people of Guyana "to help in the liberation movement of the suppressed Black people."[14] In announcing the contribution in a speech at the nonaligned conference, Burnham declared that such support would be repeated annually.[15]

The People's Progressive Party immediately stated its agreement with the contribution, commenting that it had long backed the African liberation movements. However, it called upon the PNC government to "demonstrate its sincerity by granting if not a greater, at least the same amount to the National Liberation Front of South Vietnam " The statement also asserted that

> The PPP, conscious of the fact that the separate struggles in Asia, Africa and Latin America are part and parcel of the same worldwide struggle against imperialism, supports aid for freedom fighters everywhere and this includes the Palestinian guerillas as well as those fighting the repressive regimes of Venezuela and Brazil.[16]

United Force leader Feilden Singh in a National Assembly debate on foreign policy some months later referred to the contribution as "very laudable indeed on paper," but asserted that "Those who have eyes to see will see and those who have ears to hear have heard that discrimination is rampant by the P.N.C. government in Guyana." He referred to alleged profiting from the rice industry, not by the farmers but by the "P.N.C. boys," to discrimination in the public service and in operation of the government's employment bureau, as well as to failure of the government to deliver on its promises to the Amerindians regarding their lands.[17]

In a 1972 publication, Jagan, while reiterating praise for the contribution, asserted that the donation was "part and parcel of the regime's opportunistic approach (politics, the Prime Minister once said, is the art of deals) and the means of refurbishing its tarnished anti-people and pro-imperialist image."[18]

The People's National Congress party became directly involved in African liberation efforts in 1971. A circular letter from the PNC's general secretary advised that in Guyana the party had responsibility for activities in support of World Solidarity Day, to be observed May 25, and urged financial contributions to "show our solidarity with our African brothers still under colonialism and enslavement. . . for purchasing food, medicine and arms to fight the colonialists and oppressors."[19] Posters advising of the observance featured a black figure carrying a rifle, against a barbed wire background, and requested that viewers "Give Freely for African Freedom."

Speaking at the PNC's annual delegate's conference in May 1973, Burnham declared with reference both to the PNC's contributions in relation to World Solidarity Day and the government's annual support of African Liberation Day:

> As we seek with our friends in other areas of the developing world to strengthen and make independence a reality, we cannot and must not forget the plight of those who, especially in Central and Southern Africa, still labour and slave under the imperialist yoke. There are a few reactionaries in our society who, under one guise or another, seek to question our government's annual contribution of $50,000 to the African Liberation Fund. But freedom is indivisible. We make no apologies.
>
> Further, I hope that on the 25th May our Party's contribution to the financial success of World Solidarity Day will be as outstanding as in the past. Arms and men have we none to support the Freedom Fighters, but such as we have, poor though we are, we must and shall give to see our brothers free.[20]

In August 1972, Burnham, opening the Conference of Foreign Ministers of Non-Aligned Countries in Georgetown, spoke of the linkages between developed nations and the southern African regimes toward which liberation efforts were directed.

> . . . It is the case, as we all know that there has been a sustained flow of external investments into Southern Africa. It is in the name of strategic need arising from super-power naval competition that some States now arm the Southern African regimes, and it is through clandestine trade in strategic materials that others, who adopt the rhetoric of condemnation, yet give them succour.

Identity in Transition   93

> This structure of oppression now being reinforced in Southern Africa is an alliance of the minority white Fascist and Neo-Fascist elements in the so-called white triangle. It represents a coming together into a single focus of the increasingly desperate minority elements in South Africa, Rhodesia and the Portuguese enclaves. It is more than a residual colonial situation. It has produced a series of regimes theoretically independent which, with the aid of rich covert allies, deal in human blood and misery. . . .
>
> The battle now drawn will not be won tomorrow; but there can be no doubt that the resolve of the African peoples, and other peoples despoiled of their land, will prevail. In the meantime, I submit, we must be on guard against gestures from the racist regimes which, while appearing to go a little way, are calculated to undermine our will.[21]

A new dimension in Guyana's liberation movement involvement evidenced itself in April 1974, with Georgetown as host of a four-day "International Preparatory Meeting of Indigenous Peoples." Appropriately, the conference was held in the "Umana Yana," the large structure of traditional Amerindian design erected by Amerindians for use during the 1972 nonaligned conference. Delegates and observers from Guyana, the United States, Canada, Sweden, Greenland, Denmark, Australia, and New Zealand attended. According to a report in the April 1974 *GUYNEWS,* "The meeting decided to consider the feasibility of a permanent international organization of indigenous peoples and to hold a larger conference in Canada between May and September next year."[22] The *GUYNEWS* report took some pains to assert that the conference was informed of progress in the status of Guyana's Amerindians since the British policy of treating them as "wards of the Government" and considering them "children of the forest" had been scrapped and replaced by one directed toward their integration "with the rest of the Guyanese society." Philip Duncan, an Amerindian and a Minister of State of the PNC government, was quoted as stating, after the conference had ended, that "It is clear that because of the Guyana Government's policy in respect of its indigenous peoples, Guyana cannot share all the objectives which the International Conference of Indigenous People would seek to achieve."[23]

Addressing a World Solidarity Day rally in Georgetown at the eighth anniversary of Guyana's independence, Burnham was even more explicit than he had been at the nonaligned conference two years earlier in identifying and excoriating supporters of the regimes which he viewed as oppressing blacks in southern Africa. According to a lead story in the government-owned *Sunday Chronicle,* he "bitterly denounced the hypocrisy of the big powers in Southern

Africa and called on the black people of the world 'to meet fire with fire, force with force and violence with violence.'" Further, according to the Chronicle "Mr. Burnham predicted that the success of the liberation movements in Africa was inevitable despite the assistance being given to the racist, minority, white regimes by the NATO powers." The paper quotes him as declaring "Let us hear no weeping about the violence of the African when they take their own back for [sic] their ex-oppressors!" Referring to the Mosaic law of "an eye for an eye and a tooth for a tooth," Burnham is reported to have "noted that in these days even respectable nations were meting out the Mosaic law."[24]

Social Class Aspects

Writing at about the mid-point of the nation's post-independence decade, Paul Singh of the University of Guyana's Department of Political Science viewed the country's social stratification in the following terms:

> The absence of unified pressure from the working class accounts for the inegalitarian social and economic stratification being preserved and for development being moved in the direction of greater inequality. The ordinary distribution of political power with the working class racially divided and impotent, while an upper and middle class elite of lawyers, doctors and schoolmasters rule, explains the predominance of egalitarian pretences.
>
> New incomes and new wealth are flowing into the coffers of these circulating upper middle class elites. In recent times corruption has reached fantastic proportions, tarnishing the integrity of cabinet ministers and threatening to turn the bureaucracy into a kleptocracy. There is urgent need for large egalitarian changes in the educational system, the distribution of property, the distribution of resources, the distribution of incomes from work, social manners and style of life, and the location of power within industry and agriculture. These changes taken together will constitute a major revolution. The religion of inequality and the trend towards rising inequality stand as a complex of inhibitions and obstacles to development.[25]

Archibald Singham, a political scientist who while a faculty member of the University of the West Indies in Jamaica became an experienced observer of the Commonwealth Caribbean, and N.L. Singham have attempted to depict relationships between the international system and social structures within nation-states.[26] The Singhams summarize relationships between dominant and subordinate elements of the international system in the following fashion:

> At the base level we have a dominant technological cultural system, i.e. the capacity of some cultures to more efficiently exploit the environment and to export these techniques to other societies. At the second level, the sociological level, we have a number of nation-states that play the role of classes within the hierarchical system of the dominant system, and whose internal class structures are integrally linked to the dominant system. Finally, at the ideological level, the dominant system exports its values and ideologies through such cultural devices as law, religion, education, the manipulation of folk culture by co-optation through advertising, and the arts, to overcome the resistance of national cultures to this new form of domination.[27]

Turning to black power movements in the Commonwealth Caribbean, the Singhams find them to constitute a focal point for resisting internal elite subservience to external interests:

> While the symbols and doctrines of the various black power movements in the area cannot be easily lumped together in a single, coherent ideology, in all the movements and groups there is a strong emphasis on the foreign domination and control of the economy, and the complicity of the local elites and the politicians in perpetuating this system. Since race largely coincided with class, both locally and in respect to foreign domination, this is the element largely played up in the foreign media, particularly in the U.S. and England. However, this should not be allowed to obscure the strong class and anti-imperialist basis to this type of resistance.[28]

The Singhams' focus on the concern expressed through black power movements about "the foreign domination and control of the economy, and the complicity of the local elites and politicians in perpetuating this system" provides a useful insight in understanding the relationships between internal and external social class factors and the dynamics of Guyanese politics, especially in the period since the 1968 election.

As indicated previously, Burnham and the People's National Congress party have sought to maintain a leadership position in relation to black power movements within Guyana—and even to an extent externally. Presumably among other considerations their desire was to avoid the fate that almost befell Prime Minister Eric Williams and his People's National Movement party in Trinidad and Tobago in the spring of 1970, when they came within a shade of being ousted from power because they were viewed as solidly in league with external and internal status quo elements. Thus, while Trinidad-born Stokely Carmichael was not even allowed to pass through Trinidad's airport and was barred from speaking elsewhere in the Commonwealth Caribbean, he was welcomed by Burnham to the Guyanese scene in May 1970.[29]

Burnham spoke in generally favorable tones of black power in addressing the 1969 PNC annual conference, asserting in effect that Guyana was in the process of dealing with the grievances to which the movement could, in his view, be legitimately directed.

> Some Black Power advocates, basically conscientious, look upon the movement as universally an opposition movement against all Governments. They fail to understand the real *raison d'etre* in North America and the United Kingdom and miss the core that is a quest for the recognition of the dignity of black men. In Guyana when the black man has achieved political and social gains and as a part of the society is striving towards economic power, Black Power as an opposition is self-defeating. Its role, therefore, without descending into racial fascism, is to seek to strengthen and support the social and economic revolution that is taking place here. In Guyana there is an opportunity of the black man being a real human being who does not use his new status to impose on others what he has suffered.[30]

At the April 1970 PNC annual conference, Burnham, after quoting his remarks regarding black power at the annual meeting a year earlier, perhaps to remind his audience that he did not need the events of Trinidad and Tobago to prod him into a favorable posture, stated:

> Political independence is not an end in itself but an instrument. If after its achievement no attempt is made to restructure the economy and society, if there continue to be the old white-faced cocktail parties, if foreigners continue to control the wheels of the economy and display haughty condescension towards the natives, if tokenism at the economic, employment and social levels is institutionalised then we shall all with "The white man's world of wonders"
>
>> be swallowed up in earth's vast womb
>> Or upward roll as sacrificial smoke
>> To liberate my people from its yoke!
>
> and we shall all be consumed.[31]

Slightly more than a month earlier, in addressing the conference of Pan-African and black revolutionaries held in Georgetown during Republic conversion observances, Burnham had dealt with the issue of control of the economy in relation to black power ideology, declaring:

> The Government of Guyana is not hostile to Black Power, is not afraid of Black Power, in fact, it is quite the opposite. We believe that Black Power has a contribution to make, especially here in the Caribbean. We look upon Black Power, perhaps you can tell me whether the way we look at it is the right, as a conscientious attempt by black people to stand on their own, to emphasize their identity, and to identify the links they have with black people in other countries. This, to our minds, represents both a cultural identification and, if I may use a term which may seem strange in the circumstances, an economic identification.
>
> In the West Indies, and Guyana is part of the West Indies, where black People have recently won or achieved or gained their political independence, Black Power to us means the consolidation of this political power and its being turned to good effect to achieve economic power.
>
> Those of you who were present this morning at the opening of the Guyana National Cooperative Bank will no doubt remember that I pointed to the fact that, though we have achieved political power and independence, we do not yet own our country, we do not yet control our economy.[32]

The day prior to this address, Burnham, in his speech in the National Assembly meeting inaugurating the Republic, made a clear reference to external exploitation, as well as to internal elements which, in his view, were accomplices in the process, stating:

> The people of Guyana are sick and tired of being the under dog; the people of Guyana are sick and tired of seeing their resources lying dormant, or when exploited, so frequently not for their benefit. The people of Guyana, I am sure, will take full advantage of this new phase into which we are entering.
>
> In any society, and in every period, those who have enjoyed privilege to the detriment, or disadvantage, of the many will not readily yield their positions of privilege, and there may also be others who blindly believe that having the jackal's pickings from the tables of the privileged connotes that they too, enjoy privilege.
>
> We have no illusions, Mr. Speaker. There will be opposition; there will be opposition by those who feel their entrenched positions threatened. There will be opposition by those who feel that it is better to do with the jackal's pickings rather than to look for the lion's share.[33]

Speaking to the sixth conference of heads of government of the Commonwealth Caribbean held in Jamaica in April 1970, as the drama of the black power revolt in Trinidad was unfolding, Burnham referred to "the seething ferment and incipient revolution in our midst."[34] He noted that the "young and not so young" were not satisfied merely with the region's fine weather and were concerned with "who owns what in the Caribbean."[35] He then reminded his fellow heads of government that, given their own backgrounds, they (along with himself) should be able to identify with the underclasses of the region in their demands for ending subordination to external economic interests:

> Some of us are tired of attempting to sing our songs in what has been, in fact, a foreign land. The time has come for us as leaders of our people, as men who have sprung from the gutter, as men who cannot trace their genealogies further than slavery and the proleteriat, the time has come for us to give political independence a new turn, for us to achieve economic independence in our part of the world.[36]

Burnham raised the analysis of domination-subordination relationships from the regional to the world level and urged democratization when, at the opening of the Georgetown Conference of foreign ministers of nonaligned nations in August 1972, he stated:

> Devised by the major powers after the Second World War, the present international economic and monetary system is designed primarily to serve the interests of the developed countries. In the beginning these were the interests of the industrialised West. Today this same system is now also rapidly accommodating the economic interests of other developed States as well. It is a scheme under which the economic dependence of the developing States is an essential factor in the further expansion of the wealth of the developed world. Let us not delude ourselves into believing that this system can by minor modifications be made to serve our needs. . . .
>
> Notwithstanding the limited progress that has been made in such international forums and agencies as the UNCTAD, GATT and the IMF, the economic relations between the developing and developed countries continue to be those of dependence rather than interdependence. . . .
>
> It seems that the time has now come to take clear-cut initiatives among ourselves so that we can lend our joint bargaining strength to the task of securing a *democratic* international economic system

compatible with our goals of economic independence. [Emphasis added][37]

Cultural Aspects

David Lowenthal has commented that "Submission to external cultural criteria is an inevitable concomitant of West Indian political and economic dependence."[38] He quotes Lloyd Best's assertion that "'It is accepted as natural and even desirable that the rhythm and style of life in the territory should be dominated by events in the metropolis.'"[39]

While Guyana, off the beaten track of tourism and one of relatively few nations still without a television system (and thus without "program fillers" produced in metropolitan countries),[40] is less completely within the cultural orbit of Britain, the United States, and Canada than Trinidad, or for that matter Jamaica or Barbados, the impact of the metropoles on its cultural life is, nonetheless, extensive enough.

Gordon Lewis has noted that the "pervasive feeling that Guyana is geographically and economically different from the other Caribbean lands... has tended to obscure the general truth that the historical development of the Guyanese society has been shaped by the same forces shaping the development of the island colonies—colonization, slavery sugar monoculture, the Crown Colony system."[41] Lewis points out that "There was the same diffusion of English cultural forms which made it so difficult for Guyanese, as for island West Indians, to build up the inborn sense of cultural tradition so essential to self-confidence."[42] He notes that there has been little cultural aftermath of the Dutch colonization, save in regard to the unique Dutch ability to deal with problems of water control, essential in Guyana's coastal area, along which an extensive diking system has been developed.[43]

Examples of what David Lowenthal refers to as "submission to external cultural criteria," and in some cases of clear-cut cultural dependence, were omnipresent at the time of independence. The nation's leading drama group, the Theatre Guild, founded in 1957, featured a program heavily reliant on such standards of the American and British stage as "Dial M. for Murder," "A Man for all Seasons," "Murder in the Cathedral," and "Teahouse of the August Moon."[44] The nation's leading newspaper, the *Guyana Graphic,* was foreign-owned (by Thompson Newspapers of Canada), as were the two radio services, Radio Demerara and Guyana Broadcasting Service (by Rediffusion Ltd., a British organization). Most foreign news came via Reuters, United Press, or Associated Press wire. Films were mostly from Hollywood, London, or Bombay, the latter at least representing a "developing nation" diversion. In the magazine field, such American standards as *Time, Newsweek, Ebony,* and *Life,* along with the better known British periodicals, predominated. Few books were published locally, there was no local studio for dubbing sound on film, and local printers, while capable of high-quality work, lacked the equipment necessary for some modern operations, especially in the area of color reproduction. Most school texts were created in England, often projecting an image in which white children and white adults were seen to play the dominant and attractive roles.[45] Only Christian religious occasions were observed as national holidays.[46] Of the nation's own artists and writers, many were working in foreign settings, cut off from their homeland roots.[47]

Burnham commented critically on the state of Guyanese culture at a Caribbean writers and artists conference held as part of independence celebrations in May 1966. He pledged that the government he headed would do its utmost to create an atmosphere which would encourage artists to "cease being emigres and having to go to London for recognition,"[48] and asked for ideas on the practicability of establishing a publishing company for the region "to help artists express themselves neither in chauvinism nor in the insularity that reflected colonial rule, but to show that we were on a plateau with other free people."[49] He called upon the conference to produce concrete proposals as to "what could be done to help develop an identity of our own, to discover who we are and to appreciate the area and the people of the world that is the Caribbean," proposing that Guyana host an annual Caribbean arts festival "featuring Guyanese and Caribbean artists whose work in poetry, painting and sculpture project our dreams and visions and help to foster and develop a Caribbean personality."[50]

The projected arts festival was not held until 1972, but at the next Caribbean writers and artists conference, hosted in Georgetown in connection with conversion to Republic status in February 1970, Burnham again referred to the foreign location of many area artists, commenting on the "psychological difficulty the artists must experience in singing a song in a foreign land, where he may be a monstrosity, an excrescence, an anthropological specimen,"[51] and reiterated his view of the importance of a Caribbean-based publishing house, one that would be "in its initial stages, or soon after its initial stages, owned and controlled by the people of the Caribbean."[52] Burnham then spoke of a cultural revolution, raising questions about the nature of such a revolution in terms of the search for a Caribbean identity:

> Can we bring about a cultural revolution by adopting the shibboleths and copying the postures of the very people we say we have been slaves to in the past?
>
> Can we have a cultural revolution unless we understand where we came from, what we have done and where we want to go? Is it

relevant for us to get ourselves ensnared in other people's quarrels and entangled in the differences which divide the Leviathans of the world, who use art to rationalize the power struggle? . . .

It is my conviction that the economic revolution which we plan must be accompanied by a cultural revolution, part and parcel of which is the finding of a Caribbean identity. . . .

We must decide too, what relations we should have, not merely politically or economically, but culturally with other groups in the other cultures of the world.

For instance, what must be our relationships with our black brothers in the United States of America, our brothers in Africa, and our brothers in Asia? What is the relationship between a West Indian identity and culture and the cultures of Europe and North America? Are we going to say that they are all useless, all worthless? You must provide the answer. I am a politician, you are the artists.[53]

During the post-independence decade, and especially in its latter half, a number of important steps were taken toward diminishing reliance on sources external to Guyana and the Caribbean region in the cultural realm. During the first year of independence, a holiday ordinance adopted by the National Assembly became effective, providing for observance of two Hindu and two Muslim holy days.[54] One of the two radio services was acquired by the government in 1968 and its broadcasting power enhanced to reach areas of the country not adequately serviced in the past.[55]

In early 1970 the government acquired from d'Aguiar interests the Chronicle newspaper organization, which had diminished from a daily to a weekly (Sunday) publication schedule, and re-established daily publication, seeking to challenge the Thompson-owned *Guyana Graphic's* domination in the newspaper field. In 1974 the *Graphic* was also purchased by the government.[56] The Ministry of Education began to produce a series of school books featuring art work and text appropriate to the indigenous culture.[57] Locally based printers, such as Guyana Lithographic Co. Ltd. and Autoprint, Guyana Ltd., demonstrated a capability for producing well-designed and carefully printed books.[58] In 1974 production got underway on Guyana's first full-length feature film, "The Precious Knot," filming of which was assisted financially by the Co-operative National Bank.[59]

The People's Progressive Party, while doubtless favoring, in principle, moves toward greater cultural autonomy for Guyana, viewed some of the developments critically. The Burnham government was denounced in the National Assembly for using the Guyana Broadcasting Service, the government-owned station, "for PNC propaganda," a view supported by the United Force.[60] The government was accused by PPP spokesmen, including Dr. Jagan, of discrimination in placing advertising, the assertion being that only the government-owned *Chronicle* and the PNC's weekly *New Nation* were favored in this respect.[61] The PPP also has complained that "By placing restrictions on the importation of newsprint and printing equipment, the PNC regime has severly curtailed the freedom of the press," asserting that in the period from May 1972 to May 1973 its party paper, the *Mirror,* was forced to close down three times "because of government's refusal and delay in granting licenses for the importation of newsprint" and that "During the height of the [1973] election campaign, the *Mirror* was forced to reduce its size by half and had to stop printing one day per week."[62] In 1973 the Inter-American Press Association's Freedom of the Press Committee issued a report listing Guyana as one of several countries in which the situation as to freedom of the press was "unsatisfactory."[63] The Commonwealth Press Association has apparently likewise criticized the Guyana government in this regard.[64]

Burnham's intention of shifting Guyana's cultural focus away from Britain and the United States was most clearly epitomized by sponsorship of the Caribbean Festival of Creative Arts, held in Georgetown from August 25 to September 15, 1972. Following on the heels of the conference of foreign ministers of nonaligned countries (August 8-12), Carifesta '72, as it was called, may be seen as the culmination of Burnham's efforts to foster regional development of culture, begun with the conference of writers and artists at the time of independence in May 1966 and continued with the February 1970 Republic writers and artists meeting.[65] It was apparently the largest, in terms of polities represented, broadest based Caribbean cultural gathering ever held, with dance, dramatic, musical, and other presentations not only from various parts of the Commonwealth Caribbean, but also from Haiti, Cuba, the French and Dutch Caribbean, and Mexico, to name only some of the areas represented.

Commonwealth Caribbean regional efforts to deal with the impact of foreign-owned or controlled media affecting the area, with special reference to steps called for at the Heads of Government Conference held in Kingston, Jamaica, in April 1970, have been noted in a previous chapter. The nonaligned movement, at its Algiers summit meeting in September 1973, likewise took up the question of mass media and other cultural influences from developed countries. The Economic Declaration adopted at the conference asserted, in a subsection headed "Preservation and Development of National Cultures," that

> It is recognized that the activities of imperialism are not confined solely to political and economic fields but also cover the cultural and social fields, thus imposing an alien ideological domination over

the peoples of the developing world.

The Heads of State or Government of non-aligned countries accordingly stress the need to reassert indigenous cultural identity and eliminate the harmful consequences of the colonial era and call for the preservation of their national culture and traditions.

They consider that cultural alienation and the imported civilization imposed by imperialism and colonialism should be countered by repersonalization and by constant and determined recourse to the country's own social and cultural values which define it as a sovereign people, master of its own resources so that all peoples shall exercise effective control over all their natural wealth and strive for their economic development under conditions ensuring respect for their sovereignty and authenticity, and peace and genuine international cooperation.[66]

With specific reference to mass media, the Algiers conference in the Action Programme for Economic Co-operation took the position that

Developing countries should take concerted action in the field of mass communications on the following lines in order to promote a greater inter-change of ideas among themselves.

a) Reorganization of existing communication channels which are the legacy of the colonial past and which have hampered free, direct and fast communication between them.

b) Initiate joint action for the revision of existing multilateral agreements with a view to reviewing press cable rates and facilitating faster and cheaper intercommunication.

c) Take urgent steps to expedite the process of collective ownership of communication satellites and evolve a code of conduct for directing their use.

d) Promote increased contact between the mass media, universities, libraries planning and research bodies and other institutions so as to enable developing countries to exchange experience and expertise and share ideas.[67]

Ideological Aspects

In terms of ideological development, Harold Lutchman has asserted that the Second World War was a critical period for Guyana:

The Second World War perhaps had its greatest impact at the level of ideas, and on the emergence of new forces which posed a serious threat and challenge to the *status quo*. The Nazi threat to Europe and other parts of the World resulted in some of the most pious statements in the name of self-determination as represented, for example, in the Atlantic Charter. Though after the War attempts were made to represent that the Charter did not apply to the colonial possessions of Metropolitan countries, such a stand was difficult to maintain in the face of the outstanding contribution which the colonial peoples had made in promoting the ideals of freedom. Besides, both the United States and U.S.S.R. dissented from any such limited interpretation of the matter. The result was an unprecedented questioning of colonialism.

The emergence of the U.S.S.R. as a world power also helped the reaction against colonialism. A forum such as the United Nations provided them with the opportunity of propagating their ideology and criticising the "colonial" and "imperialist" practices of the capitalist world. The U.N. was also important in another way. Once ex-colonies such as India achieved their independence, they too joined in the chorus of criticism against colonialism. In these circumstances, the demise of colonialism was only a matter of time.[68]

Lutchman comments on the impact of education abroad on the newly emerging leaders, pointing out that for Guyana, "the chief agents of hostility to British colonialism and all that it represented, were those who were fortunate enough to secure higher education overseas, whether in Europe or North America." He notes that "In many cases, during their student days after the War, they enjoyed membership of left-wing movements, some in communist parties, and generally subscribed to Marxism in some form or the other." In his view the two outstanding Guyanese examples in this regard were Cheddi Jagan and Forbes Burnham. Further, Lutchman asserts that "These persons, unlike their predecessors, were uncompromising with colonialism." They had been struck by the disparities which existed between conditions in their country and metropolitan countries, and in some instances had been victims of treatment which "emphasized the disadvantage of the colonial status, or their colour." Theirs was a demand not merely for extension of the elective principle or for sharing in the process of government, "but for full representative government, with the people's elected representatives dominating all the agencies of Government."[69]

Regarding ideological sources of the early (circa 1950) People's Progressive Party, which the Jagans, Burnham and others organized, Raymond Smith has commented that "From the beginning the party was labelled communist by the conservative press, and although this was mainly a device to discredit radicalism of any kind there is no doubt that many of the party leaders found inspiration in the writings of communist theoreticians and in the techniques of rapid economic development that they believed had been employed in countries such as Russia and China."[70]

As to the ideological orientation of the People's National Congress, Leo Despres has asserted that since the PNC was seeking, following the Jagan-Burnham split, to appeal to diverse elements of Guyanese society reflecting divergent viewpoints as to the desirability and appropriate direction of social change, its "strategy contained certain ambiguities that would make it extremely difficult to implement." the PNC wanted to mobilize support of Portuguese and what Despres describes as "other conservative elements" and, on the other hand, "had to maintain the support of the Afro-Guianese labor movement," which required that it be "critical of colonialism, of colonial institutions, of ascribed status, and of economic exploitation."[71]

In reference to the United Force party, Despres asserts that from its inception (1960) it offered "the Guianese an economic program that featured the attraction of American and British capital as the basis for economic development."[72] Charles Moskos viewed the UF as "unequivocably pro-Western in its foreign outlook."[73]

Roy Glasgow has criticized the ideological groundings of Guyanese political leaders, and, inferentially, movements headed by them, in terms of lack of indigenous roots:

> Jagan labels himself a Marxist, while Burnham conveniently
> parrots the socialist line. D'Aguiar states that he is capitalist and is
> an admirer of Salazar of Portugal. Each of these ideologies was
> never tailored to local conditions or reality. They were used for
> purposes of gaining international acceptance to suit a negative or
> positive definition of the problems. But the fact that these
> philosophies bore no relation to the Guyanese cultural milieu, served
> to make them less intelligible to the local population. Consequently,
> the leaders became "ideological colonials," imprisoned in a wall of
> international manoeuvre. The result was a complete lack of exciting,
> and inspiring symbols, which could lead to the creation of a
> common will and a more universal acceptance and participation by
> the members of the society in new beliefs and values.[74]

Gordon Lewis, in his influential study of the Commonwealth Caribbean completed in late 1967, made a comparable point. With special reference to the People's Progressive Party he said,

it is beyond doubt that the PPP record, certainly after 1955, became
a combination of 'revolutionary' Marxist utterances and unimagina-
tive action. For the PPP ideology, in truth, was an imported article
as much as the Anglo-Saxon cultural norms that, theoretically, it
attacked as imperialist. It may well be that this defect can now only
be remedied by a new leadership nurtured from 'home-grown'
Marxists as distinct from 'foreign-trained' Marxists.[75]

Speaking to a PNC regional conference in August 1969, Burnham indicated that for his party the period of coalition government had been, from an ideological perspective, essentially a holding operation:

Between 1964 and 1968 we carried out the operation of salvaging
and preserving our national assets, of restoring peace and
confidence. Not only were the attendant activities time-consuming,
but there was also the further factor of our being in harness until
November 1968 with another political party whose philosophical,
ideological and social objectives were not really coincident with our
own. It is true that we did agree on strengthening the cooperative
sector of the economy and establishing the national institution of
self-help. But a significant part of the four-year period was spent
settling differences and executing compromises in most fields.

From 1964 to 1968 our participation in government, with the
millstone of the United Force around our necks, was very much a
question of survival. That period, for us, was a holding period, we
held the foundations for improvement and movement forward later.
The time has now come for us to make that move forward.[76]

With the 1968 election behind him and the PNC firmly in the saddle, Burnham felt both the capability and the necessity for spelling out an ideological position for his party and for the nation. In theory, he had a wide range of options and models to choose from, but in fact, as suggested in the introduction to this chapter, the viable alternatives were more limited. As experienced by many Guyanese, the 1950's and 1960's had involved a traumatizing polarization in a cold war context between "eastern" and "western" conceptions of social-political-economic systems. To appear to choose either approach in charting Guyana's future would hardly constitute an avoidance of polarization or provide a basis for value consensus between the major factions in the nation. Further, there were limitations as to the magnitude of ideological shift Burnham's own party could quickly accommodate and there was a need to present, both internally and externally, an image of continuity.

The established systems of the Commonwealth Caribbean did not provide an answer. They adhered closely to the western pole in the cold war and were cast in a generally conservative mold.[77] Burnham's solution was to turn to something akin to African socialism, that is, to "socialism through cooperativism." William Friedland and Carl Rosberg have asserted that

> African socialism has a function for the African political leaders as they find themselves involved in the world conflict. It permits them to distinguish themselves from both the East and the West. It accomplishes this by delineating their role in the international arena as an independent one. Thus, African Socialism becomes equated with neutralism and other ideologies that reject political domination by either the East or the West.[78]

According to a note in his collection of speeches, Burnham in 1961 had enunciated the view that "cooperative enterprise and organization would be the instrument through which his party would establish a socialist society in Guyana."[79] To an extent, he had spelled out this approach, at the same time presenting assurances of his commitments to democracy as understood in the West, in a speech to the Washington Women's Press Club in July 1966, two months after independence:

> We believe in democracy. We believe in free and regular elections. We believe in the dignity of the individual and his right to express himself freely, but democracy does not flourish where dire poverty exists in the midst of burgeoning wealth. . . .
>
> We reject the communist dogma and system as being irrelevant and unsuited to our aspiration and needs. On the other hand, we do not see our solutions in terms of unrestricted and uninhibited free enterprise, with the government holding the ring for the exploitation of the little man who has borne the sweat and toil of the day and for whom such will mean the very negation of independence.
>
> We propose to make use of many institutional forms. There will be a place of usefulness for the foreign and local companies, the public corporation owned and controlled by the State, the joint undertaking between the State and private investors, and municipal enterprise. There will be the workers' cooperatives, producers' cooperatives, consumers' cooperatives, industrial cooperatives, and trademen's cooperatives. Participation in all these will be voluntary.
>
> It is my philosophy that the people's cooperatives, democratically controlled by the people themselves, will eventually assume an important and significant position in our economy. You may describe this as cooperative socialism.[80]

In elaborating on cooperative socialism, when in 1969 he was prepared to advance it as the centerpiece of the nation's ideological approach, Burnham emphasized the indigenous nature of the proposed orientation:

> In moving towards our goal of exploiting our resources and giving the masses economic power, we shall have to fashion new institutions, re-fashion old ones and put new content into others which already exist. The cooperative is one of the latter. It has to be expanded and adapted and given a new purpose. Investment by coops need not and must not be limited to agriculture and consumer goods but should extend into industry of all types. . . .
>
> In Guyana, it is not necessary for us to waste our time criticising one system or another practised elsewhere in the world, whether it is in the east or the west. Rather, we must spend our time doing what is best in the peculiar circumstances of Guyana. It is not our intention that, as in other countries, the cooperative movement should remain a mere appendage to the economic life of the nation. Nor is it our intention, as in the past in this country, to regard the cooperative movement as a social welfare exercise. Our basic proposition is this: the organisation of our human and material resources through the cooperative movement, with government providing financial assistance, management, training and administrative direction.[81]

In her presentation in the August 1969 National Assembly debate on the motion to declare Guyana a Republic, Mrs. Shirley Patterson, then Minister of Education, also emphasized the indigenous nature of the proposed model, asserting at the same time that this approach had support from "the people" and was not merely an implantation by the government:

> We are asked what is the model that we will use. No country can provide a model for the Co-operative Republic of Guyana. We shall cull from the experiences of other countries, we shall appropriate what has been learnt in other attempts certainly, but the model for Guyana's Co-operative Republic will come from the people themselves. It has been pushed up from below.
>
> As I said, Mr. Speaker, the significant thing about this Co-operative Republic is that there is a people and a Government who share the same philosophy, who are both socialist and who have the courage to express their socialism in a tangible form, in a realistic way in the country in which they live. This Co-operative Republic,

having come from the heart of the people itself is merely finding organisational expression through the Government.[82]

Eusi Kwayana, at the time closely associated with the Burnham government, in an essay written for a volume commemorating conversion to republic status, referred to the negative reception that the cooperative republic would receive in some circles in the United States and in the Soviet Union, and made clear his view that such reaction should be regarded in a positive light:

> Anti-democratic sources in the U.S.A. opposed to social change and black freedom are bound to see the Co-operative Republic as a new "bolshevism" or as a subtle form of communism. The U.S.S.R.'s theoreticians are bound to see it as a neocolonialist experiment. In this common ideological rejection can lie our Independence.[83]

At the April 1970 annual conference of the PNC, Burnham, in addition to distinguishing the role of cooperatives in Guyana from their role in western and eastern systems, introduced what was to become a major new element of the nation's ideological thrust—nonalignment:

> Later this year, there will be held a Conference of non-aligned nations in Addis Ababa [Lusaka became the site] at which Guyana will be represented. These nations, of which we are one, though the most numerous in the world, lack the influence even over their own affairs which their numbers may suggest. We are all the objects of control for the richer and materially stronger nations. But we possess the major portion of the world's resources—potentially. Together we can be a power and an influence if only we can identity the common objective and work to it. We cannot and should not hope to dominate others, setting up new imperialisms. The alternatives are simple—Shall we be pawns or shall we be men? And your government—the government you put into office hopes to contribute towards the correct and only real choice.[84]

After his participation in the Lusaka conference of September 1970 as head of Guyana's delegation, Burnham, addressing the April 1971 annual conference of the People's National Congress, summarized principles of the nonaligned movement and expressed PNC and governmental support, stating:

> The PNC supports all of these principles as a Party and as a Government took part in the discussions fully and subscribed to the resolutions and decisions which came out of the Conference. Our sincerity and commitment were noted as was also our financial contribution to the Liberation Fund.[85]

With the hosting of the conference of foreign ministers of nonaligned countries in Georgetown from August 8 to 12, 1972, the nonaligned philosophy was, in a sense, brought directly to Guyana. The preamble to the "Action Programme for Economic Co-operation" adopted at the meeting provided the basis for an anti-imperialist stance not necessarily anti-western in nature. In it the ministers'

> Declare that imperialism continues to be the major obstacle in the way of developing countries, and of the Non-Aligned Countries in particular, attaining standards of living consistent with the most elementary norms of human dignity. Imperialism not only opposes the proposals made by the countries of the Third World but assumes a belligerent attitude thereto, and systematically attempts to undermine its social, economic and political structures in order to maintain economic colonialism, dependence, and neo-colonialism. This state of affairs, apart from violating sovereignty and independence, takes on the characteristics of an aggression against the economies of the peoples who do not submit to its rules and dictates, going so far as to foster poverty and even wars in large areas of the world.
>
> In denouncing these facts to world public opinion the Non-Aligned Countries rely on the action of developed capitalist and socialist countries that have shown an understanding of the problems of development, to induce the community of nations to improve the efficacy of international co-operation and to defeat the purposes of imperialism.[86]

Burnham interrelated a commitment to the promotion of cooperatives within the nation with a commitment to the principles of the nonaligned movement, when, speaking to the May 1973 annual delegates' congress of the PNC, he declared:

> The emphasis on and the promotion of the co-operative is another aspect of our central philosophy of self-reliance, and our dedication to self-reliance which in turn largely inspires our membership of the Non-Aligned Movement and the role we are playing therein.
>
> Like our colleagues in that Movement, we want to be truly independent, politically and economically, like them we do not want to be pawns in the game between the major powers and blocs; like them we reject satellite status, like them we aim at owning, controlling and developing our resources for our own benefit.

> The Non-Aligned Movement, as I understand it, is not aimed at or automatically hostile to the major powers. Rather, it seeks to mobilise its members in their own political and economic interests.
>
> The task assigned to Guyana in August, 1972, after the last meeting of Foreign Ministers of Non-Aligned Countries, to co-ordinate programmes of co-operation in the fields of trade, industry and transport, as between the Non-Aligned countries and other developing countries, is a significant one. It is in keeping with the Action Programme drawn up at Georgetown and a logical concomitant to the thrust of the Movement.[87]

Burnham's approach to "socialism through cooperativism" did not lack its critics. The most trenchant critique has probably come from Paul Singh. After a closely reasoned consideration of what he refers to as "Burnhamite co-operation" (in distinction to "Jaganite Marxism/Leninism," also discussed in his article), Singh concludes:

> In the context of Guyana, co-operation thus prepares the ground for greater authoritarian control. A self elected few will exploit the simplicity, ignorance, credulity and lethargy of the overwhelming majority and dominate the co-operative societies. The entry of the movement into politics as an appendage of one particular political party seems to be poor tactics from the point of view of drawing in the whole nation. Given the conspicuous failure of the PNC to win over the East Indians, the co-operatives run the danger of limiting their clientele to members of one political party, and of transforming co-operation itself into a fascist alternative to genuine socialism. The Burnhamite version of the co-operative ideal is thus largely illusory. Moreover, the failure so far to give reality to the idea by converting the bauxite industry into a giant cooperative show piece instead of keeping it as a nationalised industry, and the failure to check the level of corruption among the co-operative societies, give added support to the contention that the new co-operative republic is seeking refuge in empty sloganeering rather than formulating a new strategy for bringing about fundamental structural changes in the socio-economic fabric of Guyana.[88]

Harold Lutchman, like Singh a member of the Political Science Department at the University of Guyana, disagreed with an earlier version of his colleague's critique, asserting "that it was not fair to condemn the co-operative to failure on *a priori* grounds, since it was conceivable that with suitable adaptations it could work in Guyana."[89]

Of the cooperative socialism proposed by Burnham, Cheddi Jagan declared in the February 23, 1970 session of the National Assembly inaugurating republic status:

> The slogan "co-operative republic" is a hoax, a fraud, to lull the Guyanese people into a false sense of security. It is a device to cloak, to hide the reality of a neo-colonialist, capitalist-imperialist republic.
>
> The truth is co-operatives cannot succeed in such an environment. They will fail here as they have failed elsewhere. Four years ago, we told them that the 7-year development plan would fail. Today, they have set it aside. The yet-to-be-born co-operative plan would also die an abortive death.
>
> The co-operatives will not bring socialism. Rather, it is only socialism which will permit the growth and development of cooperatives. In Guyana, the co-operatives will only provide the cover for a new breed of privileged capitalist elite to use the state machine to get rich quick.[90]

Jagan in effect charged "ideological subversion" by the United States when he stated in an epilogue to his *The West on Trial:*

> The University of Guyana, our high schools and government ministries are all infiltrated today by CIA spies, who pose as advisers and experts, and by Peace Corps personnel. And hundreds of thousands of U.S. books and magazines swamp our schools and libraries. The purpose is to "sell" the American way of life and the American free-enterprise or capitalist system, to gather intelligence, and to smear the PPP and socialism.
>
> Meanwhile, Guyana is having an ever-increasing stream of American evangelist crusaders, no doubt also financed by the CIA, like Billy Graham's Latin-American Crusade. The main enemy, these Christian crusaders declare, is Communism. Now and then, for good measure, they attack some of the ills of capitalism—not the system itself. All systems are bad, they add; politics and politicians cannot help the people—all the politicians have failed the people; only the return of Christ can save them. Religion in the hand of these "Sunday Christians" is made into an opiate to withdraw the people from the path of struggle for a better life.[91]

In the same work, Jagan refers to a "crisis of confidence," which he asserts "is the result of growing consciousness among the people that the PNC ruling elite, not having a principled position, moves and adopts *ad hoc* measures which are bankrupting the country."[92] In another publication, Jagan declared that "many private companies are masquerading as cooperatives and are affording the PNC ruling elite the opportunity from their exalted positions to get rich quick." In his view, "under the PNC regime, there is being created a new breed of bureaucratic capitalists who work in alliance with the foreign capitalists, and buttress the system of imperialism."[93]

Regarding allegations of "taking orders from Moscow" and "importing a foreign ideology," Jagan, in his address to the Caribbean Anti-Imperialist Conference, held in Georgetown shortly after the conference of foreign ministers of non-aligned nations, responded that "Those who take an anti-communist position and attack the Caribbean vanguard for importing a 'foreign ideology' must be told that Marxism is not a lifeless dogma, not a completed, readymade, immutable doctrine, but a living guide to action." He asserted that "some reactionary elements" would distort the feeling of national identity and pride, "turning it to nationalism and chauvinism," unwilling to admit "that it is possible and necessary to harmonize national interests with international duties." These elements, he asserted, "exploit nationalism and chauvinism to sow strife and divisions not only inside the socialist camp, but also between the socialist camp and the working-class movement of the so-called Third World."[94]

In this speech Jagan also took the opportunity of criticizing the PNC's approach to socialism through cooperatives as well as views expressed by Burnham and others regarding nonalignment. He stated that "The PNC puppet regime has declared demagogically that it is socialist and that cooperatives will be the means by which socialism will be brought to Guyana, and not vice versa as the People's Progressive Party holds, namely, cooperatives and cooperativism can succeed only in a socialist society, supplementing the dominant public sector." Citing warnings by Burnham as to self-interest of the super-powers and the necessity of third world countries coming together, as well as views expressed in various quarters as to the necessity of nonaligned countries developing their own ideology, he asserted that "These ideas are dangerous for the Latin American and Caribbean revolution; they sow illusions and divisions, and prevent the unity of all progressive anti-imperialist forces, which is so necessary for success."[95]

Eventually, with the PNC government having adopted closer ties with communist nations, having continued on its course in nationalising foreign enterprises and having, with the December 1974 "Declaration of Sophia" and other pronouncements, moved into a broader socialist stance, the basis for at least limited solidarity between the PNC and the PPP was developed, and Jagan in August 1975 announced the PPP's "critical support."[96] Speaking at a May Day rally in 1976, Burnham observed "I see my old friend Comrade Jagan taking part in a May Day parade in Georgetown for the first time certainly in two decades. We welcome the prodigal son."[97] Jagan in his address at the rally in a sense returned the sentiment, commenting:

> We welcome the assertion that the ideas of the ruling PNC are based on Marx, Engels and Lenin. Let there be from this forum, debate and dialogue on the tenets of Marxism-Leninism; at the University, this ideology must become a subject for serious study. Fundamentals of Marxist-Leninism is necessary to be known by all Guyanese.[98]

Thus the post-independence decade ended with the basis for a more indigenous and cohesive Guyanese identity established. Transitions over the ten-year period in class, cultural and ideological dimensions were probably more pronounced than were those with regard to ethnicity. The imperative, in terms of viable nationhood, for a resolution of the ethnic problem will be the focus of the concluding chapter.

Chapter 8

Beyond the First Post-independence Decade

The accomplishments of Guyana's first ten years as a nation-state were considerable and stand as a tribute both to its leadership and to its people. Inherited territory was now more securely held, regional ties considerably strengthened, global alignments more balanced, and the groundwork laid for development of an economy based upon local ownership and control and upon increasing self-reliance and third world cooperation.

However, while some progress had doubtless been made toward more cohesive societal identity, the potential for ethnic conflict remained as a major unresolved problem. For most of the period since World War II, ethnic politics were at the core of the Guyanese system. The 1968 and 1973 elections involved various techniques which assured that the People's National Congress, though substantially dependent upon a minority ethnic base, would continue in power. The possibility of building an electoral base in the Commonwealth Caribbean region, largely African in population, did not materialize, with the failure of the plan described in the "Grenada Declaration." Migration from this area to Guyana has proceeded, but not at a rate which would substantially affect the East Indian numerical superiority.

Maintenance and enhancement of power for the PNC has been largely premised upon unswerving loyalty of the centers of governmental power, namely the civil service, police and defense force. Without control of these centers, greatly facilitated by their ethnic composition, there is reason to doubt that the officially reported results of the 1968 and 1973 elections would have provided a basis for continued PNC domination. In a sense, the 1968 election results were challenged in the Rupinuni uprising, which broke out almost immediately after they were announced and which was put down only through forceful governmental response. With regard to the 1973 election, it can be noted that violence broke out even before the counting took place.

However, ethnic superiority in the centers of governmental power, though central to the Burnham-PNC strategy, was only part of the picture. Burnham and his colleagues doubtless came to realize that even if they wished to continue power relying upon the narrow ethnic base, over the long run this would not be a viable approach. The PPP, while perhaps suffering some loss of support locally following the assumption in 1969 of a clear-cut Marxist-Leninist vanguard party position, continued as an active force to be reckoned with.

With the establishment of the Cooperative Republic in 1970, the drive to achieve socialism through cooperativism, nationalization of most foreign-owned operations in the country, increasing ties with China, the USSR, and Eastern European countries, as well as with Cuba, and Guyana's participation and leadership in the nonaligned movement, a re-orientation for the PNC was apparent, closing the ideological gap between it and the PPP. Thus, since each of these parties has as its base a major ethnic segment of the country, there was movement toward national cohesion. The response of Jagan and the PPP to these approaches, by giving "critical support" in August 1975, by agreeing with the need for national unity in the face of reported external threats and destabilization efforts, and by re-entering parliament, augured well for success of the consensus approach and provided a basis for hope that the era of narrow ethnic politics, with its constant threat to the country's stabilization and development, might be coming to an end.

Yet, ethnic domination was still a reality, with the PNC continuing to exercise power through civil service, police and defense forces substantially African in makeup, and with the newly established People's Militia apparently operating from the same ethnic base. Quite possibly it was beyond the capability of Burnham and Jagan and their respective parties, given the history of struggle between them over the past two decades, to resolve this critical problem. In that event, it would remain for other figures and other movements, perhaps including the Working People's Alliance, to assure that Guyana's future, internally and as a component of the international system, would be solidly premised upon viable nationhood.

Appendix

List of Interviews*

Austin, Carl, formerly Police Commissioner.
Bacher, Steven, Officer, Cooperative National Bank.
Braithwaite, E.R., writer and formerly Guyanese Permanent Representative at the United Nations.
Burke, E., formerly Permanent Secretary, Ministry of Public Service.
Burnham, Forbes, Prime Minister.
Burroughs, Reynolds, Office of the Prime Minister.
Cameron, Norman, dramatist, author.
Campbell, Frank, formerly editor, *New Nation* (People's National Congress Party), later Ambassador to Cuba.
Campbell-Johnston, Michael, formerly Director, Guyana Institute for Social Research and Action
Carter, John, formerly Guyanese Ambassador to the United States, later High Commissioner in the United Kingdom and Ambassador to the People's Republic of China.
Carter, Martin, formerly Minister of Information and Culture, previously and later executive, Bookers Organization.
Chase, Ashton, barrister-at-law, Georgetown, and Minister of Labour, Trade and Industry in People's Progressive Party government.
Cholmondeley, Hugh, formerly Director, Guyana Broadcasting Service.
Collins, B.A.N., formerly political scientist at and Vice Chancellor of University of Guyana.
Cox, Eileen, formerly editor, *Hansard,* Parliament Office, National Assembly.
d'Aguiar, Peter, United Force leader until 1969.
Daly, Selwin, Treasurer, Transport Workers Union.
DaSilva, Elinor, United Force member, National Assembly and Chair, United Force.
Davis, Harold, formerly executive, Bookers Organization, later Chair, Guyana Sugar Corporation.
Demas, William, formerly Secretary-General, Caribbean Community, later President, Caribbean Development Bank.

---

*Positions referred to are with Guyana Government unless otherwise indicated.

Dial, Pat, formerly Archivist, National Archives and Permanent Secretary, Ministry of Information, Culture and Youth.
Field-Ridley, Shirley, Minister of Information and Culture.
Drayton, E.S., formerly Acting Secretary-General, Commonwealth Caribbean Organization.
Forsythe, Victor, Permanent Secretary, Ministry of Information, Culture and Youth.
Halder, Peter, Public Information Officer, Ministry of Foreign Affairs.
Insinally, S.R., Guyanese Ambassador to Venezuela.
Ishmael, R.A., formerly President, Trades Union Council.
Jackson, Rashleigh, formerly Permanent Secretary, Ministry of External Affairs, later Permanent Representative to the United Nations and Minister of Foreign Affairs.
Jagan, Cheddi, General Secretary, People's Progressive Party.
Jagan, Janet, Secretary for International Affairs, People's Progressive Party.
Johnson, Oscar, Director, Critchlow Labour College.
Luckhoo, Lionel, formerly Guyanese High Commissioner in the United Kingdom.
Lutchman, Harold, political scientist, University of Guyana.
MacKenzie, Clarence, formerly Director, Guyana Co-operative Union.
McCarthy, B.P., formerly President, Guyana Manufacturer's Association.
Moore, Robert, formerly historian, University of Guyana, later Guyanese High Commissioner in Canada.
Nascimento, Christopher, Minister of State, Office of the Prime Minister.
Nasseer, S.M.V., formerly President, Georgetown Chamber of Commerce.
Percival, Kenneth, formerly Acting Secretary-General, People's National Congress Party.
Pilgrim, Billy, formerly Director of Public Information, Demerara Bauxite Company.
Pilgrim, Frank, formerly Press Relations Officer to the Prime Minister.
Pollydore, J.H., General Secretary, Trades Union Council.
Ramphal, S.S., formerly Minister of Foreign Affairs and Attorney General.
Ramsahoye, Fenton, formerly People's Progressive Party member in National Assembly and Attorney General in PPP government.
Saul, Sidney, formerly Guyanese Consul, New York City, later Ambassador to Surinam.
Searwar, Lloyd, Counselor, Ministry of Foreign Affairs.
Seymour, A.J., poet, writer.
Shahabuddeen, M. formerly Solicitor-General, later Attorney-General.
Singh, Feilden, leader, United Force Party.
Singh, Paul, political scientist, University of Guyana.
Singh, Rickey, formerly journalist, *Guyana Graphic*
Stuart-Young, Brian, film producer-director, Ministry of Information, Culture and Youth.
Sutton, J.A., formerly United Force member, National Assembly.
Thomas Clive, economist, University of Guyana.

Tyndal, Joseph, formerly Chief Economist, later Secretary-General, Caribbean Community.
Venner, Noel, formerly Chief Administrative Officer, Commonwealth Caribbean Secretariat, later officer of Caribbean Development Bank.
Walcott, Clarence, officer, Co-operative National Bank.

Notes

Chapter One

1. The polity was known, until independence May 26, 1966, as British Guiana. However, Guyana is generally utilized in this study whether with regard to the pre-independence or post-independence period.
2. It is interesting to note that Guyana had been referred to by the British Guiana Commission of 1927 as "politically precocious," a description gingerly embraced by the Waddington Constitutional Commission (1951) with the comment "if this is taken to mean that there is a wide interest in political discussion we would agree." Quoted in *Report of the British Guiana Constitutional Commission 1954* (London: Her Majesty's Stationery Office, 1954, Cmd. 9274), p. 24.
3. From Dwarka Nath, *A History of Indians in Guyana,* 2nd, revised ed. (London: published by the author from 30 Crowther Rd., S. Norwood, London, SE 25 SAP, 1970), pp. 235-36, based on projections by the Registrar General.
4. *Bank of Guyana Annual Report, 1975* (Georgetown: Bank of Guyana, 1976), p. 19.
5. *Racial Problems in the Public Service: Report of the British Guiana Commission of Inquiry* (Geneva: International Commission of Jurists, 1965), Table 4, p. 165.
6. *See* Vere T. Daly, *A Short History of the Guyanese People* (London: MacMillan Education Ltd., 1975), pp. 13-21; Leo A. Despres, *Cultural Pluralism and Nationalist Politics in British Guiana* (Chicago: Rand McNally and Co., 1967), pp. 42-45; Colin Henfrey, "Guyana," in *Latin America and the Caribbean—A Handbook, ed.* Claudio Veliz (New York: Frederick A. Praeger, Inc., 1968), p. 279; Dwarka Nath, *A History of Guyana* (London: published by the author from 30 Crowther Road, South Norwood, London, SE 25 5QP, 1975), pp. 1-10; and Raymond T. Smith, *British Guiana* (London: Oxford University Press, 1962), pp. 11-13.
7. There are apparently indications of some Spanish and Portuguese explorations and settlement in the Guiana area prior even to the Dutch, but little is known of these settlements *See* Ministry of Information (of Guyana),

"Short History of Guyana," revised ed. (Georgetown: March 1969) (mimeographed document).
8. Daly, *A Short History,* pp. 41-56; Henfrey, "Guyana," pp. 279-81; Nath, *A History,* pp. 30-74; Peter Newman, *British Guiana: Problems of Cohesion in an Immigrant Society* (London: Oxford University Press for Institute of Race Relations, 1964), pp. 16-21; and Smith, *British Guiana,* pp. 13-15.
9. Newman, *British Guiana,* p. 18.
10. Great Britain, Central Office of Information, *Guyana* (London: Her Majesty's Stationery Office, 1966), p. 5.
11. Henfrey, "Guyana," p. 279.
12. Regarding the Berbice Revolt of 1763, *see* the extensive account by J.J. Hartsinck, published in Dutch in Amsterdam in 1770, translated into English by Walter Roth, Director of the British Guiana Museum, and published as appendices in the *Museum Journal* of British Guiana in eight installments in 1958, 1959, and 1960. *See also* the accounts by Pat Dial, formerly Archivist of the National Archives, Guyana, *The Sunday Chronicle,* February 22, 1970; by Daly, *A Short History,* pp. 143-52; and Nath, *A History,* pp. 79-93.
13. Smith, *British Guiana,* pp. 18-20.
14. Ibid., p. 44.
15. Nath, *Indians in Guyana,* p. 221.
16. *See* Despres, *Cultural Pluralism,* pp. 33-39; Harold Lutchman, *From Colonialism to Cooperative Republic, A Study in Political Development and Change in Guyana* (Rio Piedras, P.R.: Institute of Caribbean Studies, 1976), pp. 11-23; Smith, *British Guiana,* pp. 20-25.
17. Figures as to electorate in 1850 and 1915 from Despres, *Cultural Pluralism,* p. 39; population figures from Nath, *Indians in Guyana,* pp. 191, 231.
18. *See* Despres, *Cultural Pluralism,* p. 40.
19. Daly, *A Short History,* p. 292.
20. Ibid., pp. 292-293.
21. For discussion of this period, *see* F.R. Augier, S.C. Gordon, D.G. Hall, and M. Reckord, *The Making of the West Indies* (London: Longmans, Green and Co., Ltd., 1960), pp. 278-83; Daly, *A Short History,* pp. 293-94; J.H. Parry and P.M. Sherlock, *A Short History of the West Indies* (London: MacMillan and Co., 1963), pp. 283-84.
22. *West India Royal Commission Report* (London: Her Majesty's Stationery Office, 1945, Cmd. 6607).
23. *See* in this connection Daly, *A Short History,* p. 298; Smith, *British Guiana,* p. 164; Great Britain, Central Office of Information, *Guyana Ref. Pamphlet 71* (London: Her Majesty's Stationery Office, 1966), p.8.
24. Great Britain, *British Guiana Constitutional Commission, Report, 1954* (London: Her Majesty's Stationery Office, 1954), pp. 36-37.
25. Smith, *British Guiana,* pp. 175-78.
26. Despres, *Cultural Pluralism,* pp. 208-10.
27. Daly, *A Short History,* p. 302.

28. Despres, *Cultural Pluralism*, p. 264.
29. *See* Harold Mitchell, *Caribbean Patterns* (Edinburgh: W. and R. Chambers Ltd., 1967), p. 207; Daly, *A Short History*, pp. 304-305; Despres, *Cultural Pluralism*, pp. 264-65.
30. Mitchell, *Caribbean Patterns*, pp. 208-10. As to allegations of CIA funding of and involvement in the strike, *see* Ronald Radosh, *American Labor and United States Foreign Policy* (New York: Random House, 1969), pp. 393-405. Radosh cites *New York Times,* February 23, 1976, and *Sunday Times* (London), April 16 and 23, 1967, sources as part of the basis of his assertions.
31. Mitchell, *Caribbean Patterns,* p. 210.
32. *A Brief History,* pp. 306-307. *See also* Mitchell, *Caribbean Patterns,* p. 210.
33. Great Britain, *British Guiana Conference, 1963* (London: Her Majesty's Stationery Office, 1963), p. 4.
34. Ibid., p. 8.
35. Ibid., p. 7.
36. Ibid., p. 8.
37. Cheddi Jagan, *The West on Trial* (London: Michael Joseph, 1966), p. 389. *See,* in regard to Jagan's attitude toward independence under the then current circumstances, pp. 388-94.
38. Great Britain, *Report of the British Guiana Independence Conference, 1965* (London: Her Majesty's Stationery Office, 1965).
39. Survey on Manpower Requirements and the Labour Force by O.J.C. Francis, cited in Guyana, Ministry of Economic Development, *Second Development Plan, 1972-1976* (draft) (Georgetown: Ministry of Economic Development, 1973), pp. 53-54.
40. Barclays Bank, the Royal Bank of Canada, the Bank of Nova Scotia, and, shortly prior to independence, the Chase Manhattan Bank and the Bank of Baroda (India).
41. As of independence, the following nations maintained diplomatic missions in Guyana: Canada, India, the United Kingdom, the United States, West Germany. Since independence the West German mission has been closed and the following nations have opened missions: Brazil, China, Columbia, Egypt, Jamaica, Trinidad, and Tobago, the Union of Soviet Socialist Republics, Venezuela and Yugoslavia. The European Economic Community also maintains a mission in Georgetown.
42. Great Britain, *British Guiana—Report by the Commonwealth Team of Observers on the Election in December 1964* (London: Her Majesty's Stationery Office, 1965), p. 5.
43. *Mirror,* (Guyana), December 22, 1968, p. 1.
44. The *Sunday Times* (London), December 15, 1968, as reprinted in the *Mirror,* December 22, 1968, pp. 12-13.
45. Cheddi Jagan, *The West on Trial: The Fight for Guyana's Freedom,* revised ed. (Berlin; German Democratic Republic: Seven Seas Publishers, 1972).
46. The *New York Times,* December 22, 1968, Sect. 3, p. 6.

For discussion of procedures for and results of the 1968 election, *see* J.E. Greene, *Race vs. Politics in Guyana* (Kingston, Jamaica: Institute of Social and Economic Research, University of the West Indies, 1974), especially pp. 26-31.
47. For an official (Guyanese government) account of the uprising and allegations of Venezuelan involvement, *see* text of Prime Minister Burnham's broadcast to the nation of January 4, 1969, in his *A Destiny to Mould— Selected Discourses by the Prime Minister of Guyana* (London: Longman Caribbean, 1970), pp. 171-76.
48. *See* speech of Prime Minister Burnham to People's National Congress Regional Conference, Georgetown, August 24, 1969, quoted in Burnham, *Destiny*, pp. 152-60.
49. The *New York Times*, May 24, 1976.
50. Published by the Ministry of Foreign Affairs (Georgetown: 1972).
51. *Guyana Journal*, (Georgetown: Ministry of External Affairs), Non-Aligned Special Issue (July 1973), especially p. 88.
52. *GUYNEWS*, August 1973, p. 5.
53. "Guyana: Guided Democracy," *Latin America*, 7 (July 27, 1973), 236-37.
54. *Keesing's Contemporary Archives*, 19 (July 30 - August 5, 1973), 26016.
55. *Facts on File*, 33 (July 29 - August 4, 1973), 650.
56. Janet Jagan, *Army Intervention in the 1973 Elections in Guyana*, (Georgetown: New Guyana Co., Ltd., [1973]).
57. Quoted in Jagan, *Army Intervention*, pp. 85-86.
58. Quoted in Jagan, *Army Intervention*, p. 87.
59. *Sunday Graphic*, December 30, 1973, p. 5.
60. "State Paper on National Service for the Cooperative Republic of Guyana by the Prime Minister," presented to the National Assembly December 20, 1973 (Georgetown: Guyana Printers Ltd.).
61. *Guyana Graphic*, January 25, 1974, p. 1.
62. *Guyana Graphic*, January 28, 1974, p. 2.
63. *Bank of Guyana Annual Report 1975* (Georgetown: Bank of Guyana, 1976) pp. 100, 101.
64. Ibid., p. 9.
65. Ibid., p. 101.
66. "Budget 1977, Co-operative Republic of Guyana, National Assembly 30th December 1976" (Georgetown: Guyana Printers Ltd., n.d.), pp. 15, 20.

Chapter Two

1. *Liberator* (monthly newspaper published at Georgetown by the Guyana Anti-Discrimination Movement), June 1971, p. 4.
2. Forbes Burnham, *A Destiny to Mould* (London: Longman Caribbean, 1970), p. xiv.
3. The introduction to Burnham's *A Destiny to Mould*, written by two close

associates, Kit Nascimento and Reynold Burrows, states, in regard to Burnham's international student activities:

> A Student of Marxism, he led the West Indian Students' Delegation to the World Youth Festival in Czechoslovakia, but even then Burnham's burning sense of nationalism made him suspect and eventually reject the communist creed. To him the solution to the problem of his own people had to be found at home (p.xvii)

4. Sources regarding Burnham's background include Introduction to *A Destiny to Mould; Personalities Caribbean,* 2nd ed. (Kingston, Jamaica: Personalities Ltd., 1965); *The Queen's College Lector,* Independence Issue, May 1966, p. 3a; *Guyana Handbook 1970-71* (Georgetown: Guyana Manufacturers Association), p. 27; *Guyana in Brief* (Georgetown: Ministry of Information, Culture and Youth, 1973), pp. 7, 8.

5. In an extensive political profile on Jagan appearing in the Cooperative Republic Issue of the *Sunday Chronicle* for February 22, 1970, Guyanese journalist Mohamed Hamaludin wrote:

> Dr. Jagan tried to show that sincerity of purpose, purity of motive, need not be divorced from political astuteness at any time, even as a means to an end and this betrayed his political immaturity.
>
> Further, his political career has been marred by bad advisers, those who did not think like him, were not inspired by the same noble ideals. Because of this, it would be predicted that as soon as the people grew politically conscious—a consciousness that, ironically, *he* was to awaken—they would still hold him in respect as a good man and a good leader, but not as an astute politician. (p. 34)

6. Originally published under the title *The West on Trial: My Fight for Guyana's Freedom* (London: Michael Joseph, 1966, and New York: International Publishers, 1967), a revised edition bears the slightly modified title *The West on Trial: The Fight for Guyana's Freedom* (Berlin, German Democratic Republic: Seven Seas Publishers, 1972). All references herein are to the revised edition, unless otherwise indicated.
7. With respect to Jagan's parental background, *see The West on Trial,* pp. 11-19.
8. Ibid., p. 17.
9. Ibid., pp. 12, 14.
10. Ibid., pp. 20-23.
11. Ibid., p. 55.
12. Ibid., p. 54.
13. Ibid., p. 63.
14. Ibid., p. 64.
15. Ibid., p. 150.
16. Ibid , pp. 155-59.
17. Ibid., pp. 60-61, 97. Additional background on Jagan from *Personalities*

Caribbean and *Guyana Year Book 1967* (Georgetown: Guyana Graphic Ltd.).
18. *Guyana Year Book 1967*, p. 128.
19. Background information from *First Institute on British Guiana* (San German, Caribbean Institute and Study Center for Latin America of Inter-American University, 1964), p. 34; *Guyana in Brief* (Georgetown: Government Printing Office, 1968), p. 23; and *The Sun* (United Force newspaper), May 7, 1971, p. 1.
20. J.E. Greene, *Race vs. Politics in Guyana* (Kingston, Jamaica: Institute for Social and Economic Research, University of the West Indies, 1974), p. 45. Greene is on the faculty of the University of West Indies in Jamaica.

    Kwayana was known, until he changed his name in the late 1960's, as Sidney King.

    For background information, *see,* in addition to Greene, references in Jagan, *The West on Trial;* Leo A. Despres, *Cultural Pluralism and Nationalist Politics in British Guiana* (Chicago: Rand McNally and Co., 1967); "Confrontation Politics in Guyana," *Caribbean Contact* (Port of Spain, Trinidad), November 1976; and *Keesing's Contemporary Archives,* June 3, 1977, p. 28376.
21. *See* "Police Raid Radicals and Seize Typewriters," "Confrontation Politics in Guyana—Policy Hunting Kwayana," and "The Controversial Kwayana Trial—Diary of a Court Battle," *Caribbean Contact,* May, November, and December 1976.
22. *Dayclean,* 1, No. 7 (January 1974); 1, Nos. 14 and 15 (March 1975); 1, No. 16 (April 1975).
23. Quoted in Cheddi Jagan, "The World Communist Meeting," *Thunder,* Quarterly Theoretical and Discussion Journal of the People's Progressive Party, Guyana, 1 (October - December 1969), 54. For further information regarding the Moscow conference, *see Facts on File* for June 19-25 and June 26 - July 2, 1969
24. Jagan, "The World Communist Meeting," p. 55.
25. However, in a basic party manifesto, "Highways to Happiness," circulated in relation to the 1964 election, the United Force indicated that it favored what could be termed modernized capitalism, involving "true democracy, strong and independent trade unions, state action for social welfare, fair taxation, widespread ownership through public companies, professional management and general enlightenment" (p. 71).

    Interviews by the writer with United Force leaders in 1970 and 1971 indicated their prime concern was for the continuance of electoral democracy. Even democratic socialism was not regarded as anathema.
26. Quoted in Despres, *Cultural Pluralism,* p. 255.
27. Address of August 24, 1969, as reproduced in Burnham, *A Destiny to Mould,* pp. 155-56.
28. People's National Congress constitution as approved by the party's Special Congress held at Sophia on December 14-15, 1974.

29. *Declaration of Sophia: Address by the Leader of the People's National Congress, Prime Minister Forbes Burnham, at a Special Congress to Mark the 10th Anniversary of the P.N.C. in Government, Sophia, Georgetown, 14th December 1974* (Georgetown: Guyana Printers Ltd.), p. 16.
30. Ibid., pp. 17, 33-35.
31. *Towards the Socialist Revolution, Prime Minister Forbes Burnham at the First Biennial Congress of the People's National Congress, Sophia, 18 August 1975*, p. 10.
32. Address, as reprinted in *Thunder*, September - December 1975, pp. 26-27.

Chapter Three

1. *Guyana Journal* (Georgetown: Ministry of External Affairs), 1 (April 1968), p. 5.
2. For background on the federation and analysis of its failure, *see* Sir John Mordecai, *The West Indies: Federal Negotiations* (Evanston, Ill.: Northwestern University Press, 1968); Hugh W. Springer, *Reflections on the Failure of the First West Indian Federation* (Cambridge, Mass.: Harvard University Center for International Affairs, 1962); G.H. Flanz, "West Indian Federation," in *Why Federations Fail*, ed. Thomas Franck (New York: New York University Press, 1968); and Amitai Etzioni, "A Union that Failed: The Federation of the West Indies 1958-1962," in *Political Unification: A Comparative Study of Leaders and Forces* (New York: Holt, Rinehart and Winston, 1965). For discussion of the related Anglo-American Caribbean Commission and Caribbean Commission, predecessors of the West Indies Federation, though broader in terms of polities involved, *see* Herbert Corkran, Jr., *Patterns of International Cooperation in the Caribbean, 1942-1969* (Dallas: Southern Methodist University Press, 1970). For an outstanding collection of documents on Caribbean regional cooperation and integration, *see* Roy Preiswerk, ed., *Documents on International Relations in the Caribbean* (Rio Piedras, P.R., and St. Augustine, Trinidad: joint publication of Institute of Caribbean Studies and Institute of International Relations, 1970).
3. For background on CARIFTA and CARICOM, *see CARIFTA and the New Caribbean* (Georgetown: Commonwealth Caribbean Regional Secretariat, 1971); *From CARIFTA to Caribbean Community* (Georgetown: Commonwealth Caribbean Regional Secretariat, 1972); *The Caribbean Community: A Guide* (Georgetown: Caribbean Community Secretariat, 1973); and *One Year of CARICOM* (Georgetown: Commonwealth Caribbean Secretariat, 1974). For text of the CARIFTA agreement, as modified in 1968, *see* Preiswerk, *Documents*, pp 412-47. For text of the agreements establishing CARICOM, *see The Georgetown Accord and Treaty of Chaguaramas and Related Documents* (Georgetown: Ministry of Foreign Affairs, [1973]).

4. Forbes Burnham, *A Destiny to Mould* (London: Longman Caribbean Ltd., 1970), p. 245.
5. Forbes Burnham, "To Own Guyana: Address by Prime Minister Forbes Burnham, Leader of the People's National Congress, at the 14th Annual Delegates' Congress of the Party" (Georgetown: People's National Congress, [1971]), p. 48.
6. Signatories of the Grenada Declaration, aside from Guyana, were governments of Dominica, Grenada, St. Kitts-Nevis-Anguilla, St. Lucia and St. Vincent. The only associated state not subscribing was Antigua. The declaration was signed at Grand Anse, Grenada.
7. For text of the Grenada Declaration, *see* Press Release No.46/1971, Commonwealth Caribbean Regional Secretariat (mimeo). For background, *see News from Guyana,* No. 30/1971 (Ministry of Information, Georgetown); *Trinidad Guardian,* July 5, 1971, p. 1; *Guyana Graphic,* October 14, 1971, p. 1; and lecture by Prime Minister Burnham, "The Case for Caribbean Political Integration," delivered November 1971 and published in *The Critchlow Lectures: Some Aspects of Caribbean Integration* (Georgetown: Critchlow Labour College, [1972]).
8. Remarks in debate on March 17, 1948, in *Federation, British Caribbean Territories—Extracts from Hansard of the Proceedings of The Legislative Council, British Guiana, August 1945 to April 1953* (Georgetown: n.d.), p. 141. Eventually, in February 1953, just before the Legislative Council ceased functioning (a new body, the House of Assembly, replaced it after elections held that April), the Council voted eleven to ten, with Jagan among the minority, to send an observer to federation talks in London.
9. Remarks in debate of August 29, 1958, in *Proceedings of the Second Legislative Council* (Georgetown: n.d.), p. 1999. Burnham's resolution was defeated, in the sense that an amended version was adopted under which British Guiana's membership would be conditioned on the Federation's attaining dominion status, on Guiana's attaining internal self-government, and on approval of entry by the Guyanese people through a plebiscite. Jagan supported the amended version and Burnham opposed it. (The vote, on September 10, 1958, was nine to eight in favor of insisting that the federation have attained dominion status and British Guiana internal self-government, ten to seven on requiring a plebiscite [*Proceedings*, pp. 2184-85].)
10. Typewritten transcript of proceedings for afternoon of December 29, 1966, obtained from Office of Clerk of National Assembly, pp. 1-12.
11. Ibid., p. 2.
12. Cheddi Jagan, *A West Indian State; Pro-Imperialist or Anti-Imperialist* (Georgetown: New Guyana Co., Ltd., 1972), p. 14.
13. Ibid., pp. 22-23.
14. *From CARIFTA to Caribbean Community,* pp. 36, 37.
15. Burnham, *To Own Guyana,* p. 48.
16. *Guyana Graphic,* May 1, 1970, p. 1.

17. Segal, *The Politics of Caribbean Economic Integration* (Rio Piedras, P.R.: Institute of Caribbean Studies, 1968), p. 47.
18. Havelock Brewster and Clive Y. Thomas, *The Dynamics of West Indian Economic Integration* (Kingston: Institute of Social and Economic Research, University of the West Indies, 1969), p. 334.
19. Segal, *Caribbean Economic Integration*, p. 71.
20. *Guyana Journal* (Georgetown: Ministry of External Affairs), 1 (December 1969), 8.
21. Ibid.
22. *Evening Post* (Georgetown), February 4, 1970, p. 1.
23. *Trinidad Guardian*, July 17, 1968, p. 1.
24. *Guyana Journal*, 1 (September 1970), 94.
25. Burnham, "To Own Guyana," pp. 47-48.
26. *Guyana Journal*, 1 (September 1970), 6. This heads of government conference was held in Kingston, Jamaica, April 13-17. The Trinidad revolt, smouldering for several months, broke out a few days after the conference ended.
27. Ibid., pp. 5-6.
28. Ibid., pp. 7-8.
29. Ibid., p. 8.
30. Burnham announced in May 1969 a policy of encouraging immigration to Guyana, primarily from the West Indies, to help populate the interior (*Guyana Graphic*, May 28, 1969, p. 1).

    Temporary immigrants to Guyana whose country of usual residence was Trinidad, Grenada, St. Vincent, St. Lucia, Barbados, Jamaica or "Other Caribbean" numbered only fifty-three for 1969, according to the international migration report for that year. The report shows 182 permanent immigrants from these countries. The 1970 migration report shows fifty-five temporary and 191 permanent immigrants from these entities. See *International Migration Report 1969* and *International Migration Report 1970* (Georgetown: Statistical Bureau, Ministry of Finance). While a certain number of persons arrive from Commonwealth Caribbean polities without passing through immigration formalities, I do not believe this number to be sufficient to markedly affect ethnic proportions in the country.

    I am of the opinion that there has been no substantial upsurge in immigration from the areas mentioned since the years referred to above.
31. *The Critchlow Lectures*, pp. 13, 14.
32. Burnham, *A Destiny to Mould*, p. 246.
33. *Critchlow Lectures*, p. 11.
34. See "$800m Food Plan" and "Growing Corn and Soyabean to Cut WI's Huge $ Billion Food Bill," *Caribbean Contact* (Port of Spain), February 1976, October 1977.
35. See *Declaration of Sophia* (December 1974) and *Towards the Socialist Revolution* (August 1975).

36. "Trans-national Corporations (TNC), Their Roles and Effects with Reference to the Caribbean Common Market (CARICOM)," *Thunder,* January - March 1975; "Address delivered to 25th Anniversary Conference on behalf of the Central Committee of the People's Progressive Party by Dr. Jagan," *Thunder,* September - December 1975; Dr. Cheddi Jagan, "Imperialist Intrigue in the Caribbean," *Thunder,* January - March 1976.
37. *Ratoon,* April 1975.

Chapter Four

1. *American Journal of International Law* (1949), pp. 523-30.
2. Basil Ince, "The Venezuela-Guyana Boundary Dispute in the United Nations," *Caribbean Studies,* 9 (January 1970), pp. 13-14.
3. Article IV, Geneva Agreement of February 17, 1966, as set out in a white paper issued by the Ministry of External Affairs, Guyana, September 1968, entitled *Guyana/Venezuela Relations.*

    Venezuelan viewpoints regarding the border dispute are set out in the following documents: Venezuela, Ministerio de Relaciones Exteriores, *Report on the Boundary Question with British Guiana Submitted to the National Government by the Venezuelan Experts* (Caracas: 1967); Venezuela, Ministerio de Relaciones Exteriores, *Reclamacion de la Guayana Esequiba* (Caracas: n.p., 1967); Venezuela, Ministerio de Relaciones Exteriores, *Mensajes Presidenciales y Discursos de Cancilleres: Reclamacion de la Guayana Esequiba* (Caracas: 1967).

    For further details on background of the Venezuela border dispute, *see* Ince, "Boundary Dispute"; Cedric Joseph, "The Venezuela-Guyana Boundary Arbitration of 1889: An Appraisal," *Caribbean Studies,* 10 (July 1970 and January 1971).
4. The protocol is to remain in force for a minimum of twelve years but continues automatically thereafter for successive twelve-year periods unless either party gives due notice that it should be terminated at the end of such a period or extended for a shorter time than another twelve years (but not less than five years). *See* Article V, Protocol of Port of Spain, *Guyana Journal* (Georgetown: Ministry of External Affairs), 1 (September 1970), 90-92.
5. Protocol of Port of Spain, Article I.
6. Guyana, Ministry of External Affairs, *Friendship with Integrity: Guyana/Surinam Relations* (Georgetown: 1969), p. 10. This pamphlet, consisting largely of a speech given by Minister of State S.S. Ramphal in February 1968, provides background to the dispute from Guyana's viewpoint. *See also* Sir Harold Mitchell, *Caribbean Patterns* (Edinburgh: W and R Chambers Ltd., 1967), pp. 288-89; Albert Gastmann, "The Politics of Surinam," in *Politics and Economics in the Caribbean,* ed. T.G. Mathews and F.M. Andic (Reo Piedras, P.R.: Institute of Caribbean Studies, 1971), p. 147.

7. Statement in the Guyanese National Assembly, August 21, 1969, published in *Guyana Journal*, 1 (December 1969), 55.
8. Accounts, from the Guyanese viewpoint, of such recrimination and conflict can be found in *Guyana Journal*, 1 (April 1968), 39-41 and 1 (December 1969), 55-56; Burnham, *A Destiny to Mould*, pp. 177-79.
9. From text of communique issued at conclusion of talks between the leaders as set out in *Guyana Journal*, 1 (September 1970), 102-103.
10. Ibid., p. 103.
11. Ibid., p. 105.
12. Ibid., p. 107.
13. Ibid.
14. *Guyana Journal*, 1 (December 1971), 76-82.
15. Ibid., p. 76.
16. Ibid.
17. The treaty of arbitration, under which the boundary question was submitted to the King of Italy, and the demarcation are discussed in *Guyana Journal*, 1 (December 1969), p. 50.
18. Ibid., pp. 50-54.
19. *The Daily Journal* (Caracas), January 30, 1970, p. 5.
    For a more general consideration of Brazilian policy with regard to boundaries, *see* E. Bradford Burns, "Tradition and Variation in Brazilian Foreign Policy," in *Latin American International Relations,* ed. Carlos Astiz (Notre Dame: University of Notre Dame Press, 1969), pp. 176-77.
20. Detailed allegations of Venezuelan army support of the uprising are contained in Prime Minister Burnham's report to the nation on the incident, broadcast January 4, 1969, and published in *A Destiny to Mould*, pp. 171-76. *See* especially pp. 174-75.
21. I was in Georgetown at the time of the uprising and observed picketing in front of the Venezuelan Embassy several days later (January 9) in which placards bearing legends "UF Guilty of High Treason" and "Venezuela-United Force Responsible—Beware," among others, were carried. These legends were probably targeted more toward Valerie Hart than Peter d'Aguiar, however; Mrs. Hart, who was apparently one of the leaders of the revolt, had been a United Force candidate for a National Assembly seat in the election the previous month. She went to Caracas after the revolt, where she advised United Press International on January 6 that the intention had been to establish an autonomous state in the Rupununi area. She asserted that more than ninety percent of the 13,000 people who, according to her estimate, lived in the region supported creation of such a state (*Guyana Graphic*, January 6, 1969, p. 1).
22. Speech of May 26, 1969, as reproduced in *A Destiny to Mould*, p. 150.
23. Speech of September 15, 1969, as reproduced in *A Destiny to Mould*, p. 185.
24. *Guyana Graphic*, August 23, 1969, p. 1.
25. *Evening Post* (Georgetown), September 11, 1969, p. 1.

26. *Policy for the New Co-op Republic, Addresses to the 13th Annual Conference of the People's National Congress, April 2-8, 1970* (Georgetown: People's National Congress, 1970), p. 21.
27. Typewritten transcript of debate of February 28, 1964, obtained from The Parliament Office, p. 3.
28. Typewritten transcript of debate of July 17, 1968, obtained from The Parliament Office, p. 29.
29. "Agreement Between Great Britain and Venezuela concerning the Procedure for Resolving the Boundary Dispute Over Guyana," signed February 17, 1966, Geneva, Switzerland, as reproduced in *Documents on International Relations in the Caribbean,* ed. Roy Preiswerk (Rio Piedras, P.R.: Institute of Caribbean Studies, and St. Augustine, Trinidad: Institute of International Relations, University of the West Indies, 1970), p. 714.
30. Typewritten transcript of debate of July 17, 1968, obtained from The Parliament Office, p. 15.
31. Ibid., p. 17.
32. Ibid., p. 17; also quoted in the pamphlet "Border Conspiracy Exposed by Cheddi Jagan" (People's Progressive Party, November 1968), p. 8.
33. *Mirror,* June 21, 1970.
34. Typewritten transcript of Jagan's National Assembly statement of June 22, 1970, obtained from The Parliament Office, pp. 4-5.
35. "Guyana/Venezuela Relations" (Georgetown: Ministry of External Affairs, September 1968), pp. 67-68.
36. *Sunday Graphic,* September 7, 1969.
37. *Guyana Journal* 1 (December 1968), pp. 57-59. The full text of the presidential decree is reproduced in Preiswerk, *International Relations,* pp. 718-19.
38. *Guyana Journal,* 1 (December 1968), 57-59.

    With regard to the decree, S.S. Ramphal, addressing the United Nations General Assembly, October 3, 1968, declared:

    On 9th July of this very year, the President of Venezuela issued a decree in which he purported to annex as part of the territory of Venezuela, and to assert a right to exercise sovereignty over a 9-mile belt of sea extending to within three miles of the coast of Guyana and contiguous to Guyana's territorial waters. The decree is a manifest absurdity which my Government has repudiated for the nullity that it is. But perhaps most significant of all for this Assembly is the way in which it seeks to overthrow some of the fundamental principles underpinning the International Conventions on the Law of the Sea, which were the outcome of a major United Nations effort aimed at defining and consolidating the principles of international law governing the territorial sea, the contiguous zone, the continental shelf, the regime of the high seas and fishery conservation. (S.S. Ramphal, "Development or Defence: The Small State Threatened with Agression" [Georgetown: Ministry of External Affairs, December 1968], p. 10.)

39. *Daily Journal* (Caracas), February 1, 1970, p. 1. The *Daily Journal's* correspondent also referred to an American-owned manganese mining operation that had been closed down in the disputed territory (presumably at Matthew's Ridge in the Northwest region). Opinions were in conflict as to whether Venezuelan pressures on the company involved (Union Carbide) or depletion of the manganese deposits had caused the termination of operations. (*Daily Journal*, February 2, 1970, p. 6.)

40. Article II of the Protocol provides:

> (1) So long as this Protocol remains in force no claim whatever arising out of the contention referred to in Article 1 of the Geneva Agreement shall be asserted by Venezuela to territorial sovereignty in the territories of Guyana or by Guyana to territorial sovereignty in the territories of Venezuela.
>
> (2) In this Article, the references to the territories of Guyana and the territories of Venezuela shall have the same meaning as the references to the territories of British Guiana and the territories of Venezuela respectively in the Geneva Agreement. (*Guyana Journal* [September 1970], 90.)

41. *Guyana Journal*, 1 (December 1969), 133-34.
42. Burnham, *A Destiny to Mould*, 179.
43. *Policy for the New Co-op Republic*, p. 90.
44. "Report to the Nation by the Prime Minister," n.d., p. 2 (mimeographed document).
45. Speech to open air meeting in Georgetown on third anniversary of independence, May 26, 1969, reproduced in Burnham, *A Destiny to Mould*, pp. 150-51.
46. K.F.S. King, Minister of Economic Development, "Regional Inputs: The Second Development Plan—1972-76," in "A Great Future Together," 16th Annual Congress of People's National Congress, May 8, 1973, pp. 23-28.
47. "State Paper on National Service for the Cooperative Republic of Guyana by the Prime Minister," presented to the National Assembly December 20, 1973 (Georgetown: Guyana Printers Ltd., n.d.), pp. 10-11.
48. Population figures from Dwarka Nath, *A History of Indians in Guyana*, 2nd revised ed. (London: published by the author from 30 Crowther Rd., S. Norwood, London, S.E. 25, 1970), Table 5 (based upon Registrar General's estimates), pp. 235-36. While Nath's study is devoted to the East Indians of Guyana, not the Amerindians, its presentation of population and other statistics is extensive.

    It is noteworthy that Guyana's Amerindian population has increased over the years, from approximately 7,500 in 1891, to some 16,700 in 1949, to 25,450 in 1960 and to about 32,000 in 1968.

49. The famous Trinidad novelist V.S. Naipaul in *The Middle Passage—The Caribbean Revisited* (London: Andre Deutsch, 1962) comments, in regard

to his visit to the Guyanese interior, that "Everyone knows that Amerindians hunted down runaway slaves; it was something I heard again and again, from white and black; and on the Rupununi, and wherever one sees Amerindians, it is a chilling memory" (p. 99).
50. Burnham, *A Destiny to Mould*, p. 174.
51. Typewritten transcript of debate of July 17, 1968, obtained from Office of Clerk of National Assembly, p. 28.
52. "Report of the British Guiana Independence Conference, 1965" (London: Her Majesty's Stationery Office, n.d.) Annex C, p. 20.
53. *Mirror*, February 4, 1970.
54. *Mirror*, February 3, 1970.
55. Dr. Cheddi Jagan, as Leader of the Opposition, protested in the National Assembly on February 9 what he asserted was a violation of Amerindian civil rights during the conference. According to Jagan, Amerindians who attempted to picket on the pavement outside the Public Buildings where the conference was held were relieved of the protest signs by police. (*Mirror*, February 10, 1970, p. 1; *see also Mirror*, February 8, 1970, p. 1).
56. *Sunday Graphic*, February 8, 1970, p. 1; *New Nation*, February 8, 1970, p. 1.
57. *Guyana Graphic*, February 7, 1970, p. 1.
58. *GUYNEWS*, No. 3 (1976), p. 4.
59. Amerindian (Amendment) Act 1976, passed by National Assembly April 5, 1976, approved by President Chung April 21, 1976.
60. "9,000 Sq. Miles of Land for Guyana's Amerindians," filed from Georgetown by Hubert Williams, *Caribbean Contact* (Port of Spain, Trinidad), April 1976, p. 17.
61. Ibid. According to Williams, the Amerindians are the fastest growing ethnic group in Guyana, averaging 3.2 percent a year, compared with the national average of 2.3 percent. He states that "Census figures here show them at 16,300 in 1946, 25,453 in 1960 and 31,460 at independence in 1966. The Census of 1970 had them at 43,412 and government says the figure now reached 50,000."
62. *Daily Journal* (Caracas), February 3, 1970, p. 4.

As of independence, the Defence Force numbered about 500, with a volunteer batallion of 200. However, according to a release issued at that time, it was to be "1,000 strong at the end of the year and will build up to full strength [unspecified] next year." ("Guyana Defence Force—Middlesex Regiment Staying on to Help Training," mimeographed one-page release, undated but apparently issued just prior to independence).
63. Ibid. An indication of continued British involvement in training for the Guyana Defence Force is provided by an article in the December 1975 issue of *Green Beret*, the Force's newspaper, reporting on the return of a GDF officer following course completion at a military staff college at Camberley, Surrey. The same issue reports on return of another officer from staff college training in Canada.
64. *Draft, Second Development Plan, 1972-1976* (Georgetown: Ministry of Economic Development, [1973]), p. 149.

65. Ibid., p. 150. For discussion of farming operations being carried out by the Guyana Defence Force, *see* "GDF farms make national contribution," *Green Beret*, December 1975. (Guyana Defence Force Education Unit).
66. *Draft, Second Development Plan, 1972-1976* (Georgetown: Ministry of Economic Development, [1973]), p. 149.
67. *GIS News* (Georgetown: Ministry of Information and Culture), March 4, 1976, and *Hydro-Focus* (Georgetown: Upper Mazaruni Development Authority), May 26, 1976.

In a message recorded for Guyanese residing overseas at the time of tenth anniversary of independence celebrations, Burnham asserted that it had been possible to "maintain our current schedules for the implementation of a major hydroelectric facility capable of generating somewhat over 3000 megawatts by 1980-81." *News Release* (Embassy of the Republic of Guyana, Washington, D.C.), May - June 1976.

Chapter Five

1. Roy Preiswerk, "The New Regional Dimensions of the Foreign Policies of Commonwealth Caribbean States," in *Regionalism and the Commonwealth Caribbean*, ed. Roy Preiswerk (St. Augustine, Trinidad: Institute of International Relations, University of the West Indies, 1969), p. 9. Preiswerk, a Swiss international lawyer and international relations specialist, was director of the Institute of International Relations when he edited the volume just cited, which was based upon a series of lectures sponsored by the Institute.
2. Cheddi Jagan, *The West on Trial: The Fight for Guyana's Freedom* (Berlin, German Democratic Republic: Seven Seas Publishers, 1972), pp. 198, 228. As to rice sales to the U.S.S.R., *see* Ernst Halperin, "Racism and Communism in British Guiana," *Journal of Inter-American Studies,* III (January 1965), 97.
3. Jagan, *The West on Trial*, p. 191. The assistance offered totalled over US $20 million in value.
4. Ibid. "No doubt, the Colonial Office consulted the Foreign Office," Jagan states, "which then consulted the U.S. State Department. I was finally told that a great deal more work had to be done to find out if the project would be economically feasible!" (Ibid.).

As to the Hungarian glass factory, a series of delays and maneuvers, involving an adverse opinion on economic feasibility by a United States International Cooperation Administration official and roadblocks on financing and equipment availability, are cited (ibid., p. 190). In regard to the rice-barn oil factory, Commonwealth Development Corporation objections are referred to, although their nature is not clear and they were apparently eventually overcome (ibid., pp. 190-191).
5. Ibid., p. 191.
6. Ibid., p. 192.

7. Arthur M. Schlesinger, Jr., *A Thousand Days: John F. Kennedy in the White House* (London: Andre Deutsch Ltd., 1965), pp. 667-68.
8. Ibid., pp. 668, 669.
9. Ronald Radosh, *American Labor and United States Foreign Policy* (New York: Random House, 1969), pp. 402-404. For further discussion of CIA and American labor involvement in pre-independence Guyana, *see* pp. 393-405, and Colin V.F. Henfrey, "Foreign Influence in Guyana: The Struggle for Independence," in *Patterns of Foreign Influence in the Caribbean,* ed. Emanuel de Kadt (New York and London: Oxford University Press, 1972), pp. 68-73.
10. Sir Cameron Mitchell, *Caribbean Patterns: A Political and Economic Study of the Contemporary Caribbean* (Edinburgh and London: W. and R. Chambers Ltd., 1967), p. 227.
11. Forbes Burnham, *A Destiny to Mould* (London: Longman Caribbean, 1970), pp. 193-94.
12. Ibid., p. 194.
13. Ibid.
14. Ibid., p. 194.
15. Ibid., p. 195
16. Press release, "President Johnson sends Personal Independence Gift to Prime Minister Burnham of Custom-Made Western Saddle," May 25, 1966 (mimeographed document).
17. "Press Release—Atkinson Field" (Office of the Prime Minister), p. 1.

    The ninety-nine year lease to the area on which Atkinson Field was constructed had been acquired under the agreement of March 27, 1941, between the United States and Great Britain affecting many areas under British control in the Western Hemisphere. For text of the agreement, *see* Roy Preiswerk, ed., *Documents on International Relations in the Caribbean* (Rio Piedras, P.R.: Institute of Caribbean Studies, University of Puerto Rico, 1970), pp. 596-605.

    Once developed, Atkinson Field became Guyana's primary international and domestic airport. It is now known as Timeri International Airport, Timeri being an Amerindian word meaning "rock painted."

    Presumably the United States and Guyana both wished to avoid the sort of controversy which had developed in the late 1950's in Trinidad over a large naval base, known as "Chaguaramas," located near Port of Spain. In that instance, the U.S. eventually gave way, entering into a modification of the 1941 lease agreement with Great Britain. For background on the Chaguaramas controversy, *see* extract from speech by Dr. Eric Williams of July 17, 1959, "From Slavery to Chaguaramas," and text of the February 10, 1961 agreement between the U.S. and United Kingdom in Preiswerk, *Documents,* pp. 613-37.

    In June 1977 Guyana and the United States agreed to a termination of U.S. rights to Atkinson Field (Timeri International Airport). (*Keesing's Contemporary Archives,* Dec. 16, 1977, p. 28728.)

18. *Mirror* (Guyana), May 22, 1966.
19. Burnham, *A Destiny to Mould*, p. 208.
20. Ibid., p. 210.
21. Ibid.
22. Cheddi Jagan, "A Review of Guyana's Foreign Policy," *International Affairs Quarterly* (Georgetown), first independence issue, 4: 67. Reprinted in Preiswerk, *Documents*, p. 62.
23. Preiswerk, *Documents*, p. 63.
24. Ibid., p. 63.
25. Ibid., p. 65.
26. Ibid.
27. *The Constitution of Guyana and Related Constitutional Instruments* (Georgetown: Government Printery, 1966), Article 30.
28. Ibid., Article 73 (5).
    Thomas Franck has spoken of phases of independence which British colonies traditionally pass through, with the initial stage one "during which it continues to owe allegiance to the Crown as head of state." See Franck, "Some Legal Problems of Becoming a New Nation," *Columbia Journal of Transnational Law*, 1 (1965), 15.
29. Burnham, *A Destiny to Mould*, p. 65.
30. *Report of the British Guiana Independence Conference 1965* (London: Her Majesty's Stationery Office, 1965), p. 6; Cheddi Jagan, *The West on Trial*, pp. 333-39.
31. "Tell the People—Point of United Force Policy for Party Workers" (Georgetown: Daily Chronicle Ltd., [1968]), p. 7.
32. Burnham, *A Destiny to Mould*, p. 67.
33. Ibid., pp. 68, 69.
34. For text of the 1925 trade agreement and materials pertaining to Canadian aid programs in the Commonwealth Caribbean, see Preiswerk, *Documents*, pp. 111-38. For a study of trade and other aspects of Commonwealth Caribbean-Canadian links, see *West Indian-Canada Economic Relations— Selected Papers Prepared by the University of the West Indies in Connection with the Canada-Commonwealth Caribbean Conference July 1966* (Kingston, Jamaica: Institute of Social and Economic Research, University of the West Indies, 1967).
35. D.A.G. Waddell, *The West Indies and the Guianas* (Englewood Cliffs: Prentice Hall, 1967), p. 29.
36. For background on the Sir George Williams affair and its aftermath, see Dennis Forsythe, ed., *Let the Niggers Burn* (Montreal: Black Rose Books—Our Generation Press, 1971), especially "By Way of Introduction: The Sir George Williams Affair" by the editor and "The West Indies and the Sir George Williams Affair: An Assessment" by Carl Lumumba. Lumumba asserts that "Prior to the 'Affair', Canada and Canadians bore an untarnished reputation in the West Indies. . . . Subsequently, it was shown to the people how a charge of racism in a White Canadian

university was related to them, the exploited." (pp. 175, 178).

Eventually Cheddi Jagan Jr. and fellow Guyanese student Maurice Barrow, along with some others of those accused in the affair, pled guilty. Jagan and Barrow were each fined $1,000 (Canadian) and bonded to hold the peace for a period of six months at the sum of $500 (*Mirror,* September 9, 1970, p. 1).

Since the 1969 incident, Sir George Williams University has merged with another institution, the resulting entity being known as Concordia University.

37. Forbes Burnham, *To Own Guyana: Address by Prime Minister Forbes Burnham, Leader of the People's National Congress, at the 14th Annual Delegates' Congress of the Party* (Georgetown: People's National Congress, [1971]), p. 48.
38. "Canada and the Caribbean: The Alcan Story" (Montreal: Aluminum Limited, n.d.), p. 3.
39. Based upon article by "Profile Reporter," "Demba: Key to Industrial Progress," *Profile* (Georgetown), December 1968, p. 7. For early history of the Alcoa operations in Guyana, *see* Norman Girvan, "The Denationalization of Caribbean Bauxite: Alcoa in Guyana," *New World* (Kingston, Jamaica), 5, 35-48.
40. C.H. Grant, "Political Sequel to Alcan Nationalization in Guyana: The International Aspects," *Social and Economic Studies,* 22 (June 1973), 267.
41. *The Area Handbook for Guyana* (1969) states that "All of Guyana's alumina [a bauxite product] and 85% of its bauxite is produced by the Demerara Bauxite Company Ltd. (Demba). The remainder is produced by Reynolds Metals Company" (p. 215). Reynolds operations in Guyana commenced in 1952.
42. *See* in this connection H.J.M. Hubbard, *Race and Guyana* (Georgetown: H.J.M. Hubbard, 1969), p. 25, and C.H. Grant, "Company Towns in the Caribbean: A Preliminary Analysis of Christianburg-Wismar-Mackenzie," *Caribbean Studies,* 11 (April 1971), 46-72.

See also Maurice St. Pierre, "Industrial Unrest in Mackenzie, Guyana," in *McGill Studies in Caribbean Anthropology,* ed. Frances Henry (Montreal: McGill University Centre for Developing Area Studies, 1969), pp. 65-80. St. Pierre states that, while Demba had a policy of hiring Guyanese for staff positions when vacancies arose, as of July 1, 1967 there were fifty-nine Guyanese staff members (referring apparently to management level positions) in a total staff population of 165 (p. 76).

The Christianburg-Wismar-Mackenzie area, focal point of Demba mining and processing operations, was renamed Linden following the nation's independence, utilizing the first name of Prime Minister Burnham.
43. For details, from the Guyana government perspective, of the breakdown of talks with Alcan regarding governmental participation, *see* "The Nationalization of the Demerara Bauxite Co., Ltd.," in *Industrial Review* (Georgetown: Guyana Development Corp., n.d.), pp. 4-14.

For background as to the economics of the aluminum industry in reference to bauxite operations in developing countries, written by a key adviser to the Guyana government in negotiations for participation in ownership and in the eventual nationalization, see Norman Girvan, "Regional Integration vs. Company Integration," in *Caribbean Integration: Papers on Social, Political and Economic Integration,* ed. Sybil Lewis and Thomas Mathews (Rio Piedras, P.R.: Institute of Caribbean Studies, University of Puerto Rico, 1967), pp. 101-18; *see also* Girvan, "Multinational Corporations and Underdevelopment in Mineral-Export Economies," *Social and Economic Studies,* 19 (December 1970): 490-526; Girvan, "Why We Need to Nationalize Bauxite, and How," in *Readings in the Political Economy of the Caribbean,* ed. Girvan and Jefferson, pp. 217-40; and Girvan, "Making the Rules of the Game: Company-Country Agreements in the Bauxite Industry," *Social and Economic Studies,* 20 (December 1971). *See also* V.A. Lewis, "Comment on Multinational Corporations and Dependent Underdevelopment in Mineral Export Economies," *Social and Economic Studies,* 19 (December 1970), 527-33; and Raymond Vernon, "Foreign Enterprises and Developing Nations in the Raw Materials Industries," *American Economic Review* (Papers and Proceedings of the Eighty Second Annual Meeting of the American Economics Association, New York City, December 1969), LX (May 1970), 122-26.

44. "The Negotiations between the Government of Guyana and the Aluminum Company of Canada Leading to the Purchase of Alcan's Assets in Guyana and the Establishment of GUYBAU" (issued by Guyana Bauxite Company, n.d., p. 3).
45. *Guyana Journal* (Georgetown: Ministry of External Affairs), 1 (September 1970), 80.
46. *Lusaka Declaration on Peace, Independence, Development, Cooperation and Democratisation of International Relations and Resolutions of the Third Conference of Heads of State or Government of Non-Aligned Countries* (Lusaka: Ministry of Foreign Affairs, 1970), pp. 25, 26.
47. *Lusaka Declaration,* Addendum, pp. 33-48.
48. *Main Documents Relating to Conferences of Non-Aligned Countries from Belgrade, 1961 to Georgetown, 1972* (Georgetown: Ministry of Foreign Affairs, 1972), p. 105.
49. Ibid., p. 121.
50. Ibid., p. 120.
51. *Guyana Journal,* Non-Aligned Special Issue, 1 (July 1973), 90.
52. *Proposal for an Inter-Regional Project on Co-operation Among Developing Countries in the Fields of Trade, Industry and Transport, Presented by the Government of Guyana, August 1973* (mimeographed document).
53. *Documents of the Fourth Conference of Heads of State or Government of Non-Aligned Countries* (Algiers), United Nations General Assembly Document A/9330 (November 22, 1973), p. 66.

54. Ibid., p. 96. The mandate of Guyana and the other nations responsible for coordinating studies was extended to the next heads of state conference.
    At the next nonaligned nations heads of state meeting held in Colombo, Sri Lanka, August 1976, Guyana was again active, with Burnham the only head of government of a Commonwealth Caribbean nation-state attending. Elected one of the vice-presidents and chairing a plenary session, in his address to the conference he drew attention to Guyana's continuing work with regard to cooperation in trade, industry and transport. (*GUYNEWS* [Georgetown: Ministry of Information], No. 6 [1976].).
55. *Guyana Journal,* 1 (December 1971), 99.
56. *Mirror,* December 29, 1970, p. 2.
57. *Guyana Graphic,* July 6, 1972, p. 1, and Donald A.B. Trotman, *Guyana and the World* (Georgetown: United Nations Association of Guyana, 1973), p. 14.
58. *GUYNEWS,* Nov. 5, No. 4 (February 1975). Guyana's trade with Taiwan was cut off in May 1976. The Ministry of Information release announcing the termination stated "In pursuance of its policy to provide Guyanese with reasonably priced goods, Guyana has established bilateral trade agreements with the People's Republic of China; and these agreements require a certain balance of trade between the two countries to be maintained." (*News from Guyana,* May 15, 1976.)
59. *GUYNEWS,* No. 5 (1976).
60. *Pictorial Review of Prime Minister Forbes Burnham's Visits to China, Cuba and Romania* (Georgetown: Office of the Prime Minister, n.d.), p. 38.
61. "Politics of Two Men in a Divided Land," *Caribbean Contact,* September 1975.
62. *See* "Cuban Doctors for Guyana," *GIS News* (Ministry of Information and Culture), March 1, 1976, and "Health Teams for Cuba," *GIS News,* May 3, 1976.
63. *Caribbean Monthly Bulletin* (Institute of Caribbean Studies, University of Puerto Rico) (November - December 1973), p. 5.
64. *GIS News,* May 17, 1976.
65. *GUYNEWS,* April 1974.
66. *Caribbean Monthly Bulletin* (June 1977), p. 32.
67. *GUYNEWS,* No. 6 (1976). In May 1976 the Soviet Trade Union Council offered study opportunities in the U.S.S.R. for Guyanese. *GIS News,* May 19, 1976.
68. *Keesing's Contemporary Archives,* October 1, 1976, p. 27972.
69. Ibid. The Keesing's report notes that the *Resumen* claim "was not substantiated when journalists were invited to visit the areas concerned."
70. *Guyana Chronicle,* February 23, 1976, p. 1.
71. *Caribbean Monthly Bulletin,* April 1976, p. 14.
72. *The Sunday Graphic* (Guyana) of March 21, 1976 had reported that Venezuelan President Carlos Andres Peres had "received with satisfaction"

140   Guyana Emergent

assurances from Guyana that it would not allow itself to be used to spread discord in Latin America or for international subversive operations. In a tenth anniversary of independence greeting, Venezuela's ambassador in Georgetown asserted that "History will record Guyana's first ten years of independence as the period when the Republic of Guyana, not unlike my own country under the leadership of Carlos Andres Peres, boldly advocated and struggled for a new international economic order." (*GIS News,* May 22, 1976).

In July 1976 Foreign Minister Wills paid what was referred to as a "cordial" visit to Brazil, where he was received by President Ernesto Geisel. Speaking in reply to an address of welcome by his Brazilian counterpart, Wills stated that he wished to "indicate how ridiculous must be the rumour spread within the last several months by the international press that Guyana is aggressive towards her neighbours in Venezuela and Brazil. . . . Guyana has neither the capacity nor the desire nor indeed the reason to be aggressive to anyone, least of all her neighbours." (*Guyana Newsletter* [Office of the High Commissioner for Guyana to Canada], September 1976, pp. 6, 7). The foreign ministers exchanged notes looking to establishment of a Brazil-Guyana Joint Commission to integrate cultural and economic relations (ibid.).

Regarding markedly improved U.S.-Guyana relations as an aspect of Carter administration policy, *see* "Caribbean: Friends and Neighbours," *Latin America Political Report* (London), August 5, 1977; "Young Spearheading a Good-Will Mission," *New York Times,* August 14, 1977, p. 15; and "Warming Up to the Islands in the Sun" (editorial), *New York Times,* August 26, 1977, p. A20.

73. A senior official of Guyana's foreign affairs establishment pointed out to me in January 1969 the necessity for his country maintaining a "status-quo" orientation while the territorial claims remained unresolved.
74. "Guyana's Foreign Policy in Healthy State," *Guyana Chronicle,* May 26, 1976.
75. Clive Thomas, "Bread and Justice: The Struggle for Socialism in Guyana," *Monthly Review,* September 1976.
76. Basil Ince, "The Caribbean in World Politics" (January 22, 1974), p. 18 (mimeographed document). Ince, a Trinidad-born political scientist, has been a member of the faculty of the Institute of International Relations of the University of the West Indies, Trinidad, since 1972.

Chapter Six
1. William G. Demas, *The Economics of Development in Small Countries with Special Reference to the Caribbean* (Montreal: McGill University Press, 1965), p. 115. This publication is based upon the Collard Lectures which Demas delivered at McGill University in March 1964. At that time, he was on leave from his position as head of the Economic Planning Division of the government of Trinidad and Tobago for a five-month stint as the

first research fellow at McGill's newly established Centre for Developing-Area Studies. Demas became Secretary-General of the Commonwealth Caribbean Regional Secretariat in January 1970 and took up duties as president of the Caribbean Development Bank in the fall of 1974, succeeding another prominent Commonwealth Caribbean economist, W. Arthur Lewis, in that post. The impact of *Economics of Development in Small Countries* can be judged from its printing history, involving a reprinting in 1966, a paperback edition in the same year, and a further reprinting in 1969.

2. Ved P. Duggal, "Guyana, Economic Development Since Independence," in *Guyana: A Composite Monograph,* ed. Brian Irving (Hato Rey, P.R.: Inter American University Press, 1972), p. 56.

   According to a ten-year economic review presented in Guyana's 1966-72 development plan, during the 1954-64 period, "A large proportion (just over half) of investment funds has come from abroad. Direct investment by overseas firms, including profits reinvested but excluding depreciation, accounted for 24 per cent of net capital formation, and government loans and grants from abroad accounted for 26 per cent" (*British Guiana (Guyana) Development Programme (1966-72)* [Georgetown: The Government Printery, 1966], Chapter 1, p. 6).

3. Forbes Burnham, Preface, in *British Guiana (Guyana) Development Programme (1966-1972),* p.v. Burnham's preface is dated February 1966.

4. At the conversion rate prior to devaluation of sterling in November 1967, this would be equivalent to approximately US $172 million. (Before the 1967 sterling devaluation, the U.S. dollar was equivalent to 1.71 Guyana dollars.) In 1975 Guyana's dollar was linked to the U.S. dollar. As of October 9 of that year the Guyanese/U.S. dollar rate was fixed at G$2.55 = US$1.00. (*Bank of Guyana Report, 1975* [Georgetown, Bank of Guyana, 1976], p. 44.)

5. "Ministerial Paper, Financing the Development Plan", in *British Guiana (Guyana) Development Programme (1966-1972),* p. 6.

6. Forbes Burnham, Preface, *British Guiana (Guyana) Development Programme (1966-1972),* pp. vii-viii.

7. Ibid., p. viii.

8. *Bank of Guyana Report, 1975,* p. 98.

9. *Second Development Plan 1972-1976, Government of the Cooperative Republic of Guyana* (Georgetown: Ministry of Economic Development, 1973), p. 161. The version of the plan referred to herein is labeled on its cover "Draft" and is in mimeographed form. The $748 million from domestic savings and $413 million from external resources total $1161 million, or $10 million more than the overall goal of $1151 million, an apparent error in the draft presentation.

   For an extremely useful comparison of post-World War II development plans in Guyana, including a ten-year program (1947-56), a five-year program (1954-58) recommended in an International Bank for Reconstruction and Development report, a five-year program (1960-64) based upon recommendations of Cambridge University economist Kenneth Berrill, and the seven-year program (1966-72) drawn up by the group headed by W. Arthur Lewis, see Wilfred L. David, "Economic Planning in Guyana—Historical Review and Evaluation," in *Caribbean Development and the Future of the Church* (Georgetown: Guyana Institute for Social Research and Action, 1969). David, a Guyanese economist who was for a time a University of Guyana faculty member, was in charge of development of the 1972-76 plan until he was succeeded in August 1970 by Winston King, then the Guyana government's chief planning officer (*Mirror,* August 18, 1970, p. 1).

10. *British Guiana (Guyana) Development Programme (1966-1972),* Chapter Three, pp. 4-5.
11. Ibid., p. 5.
12. For an assessment of utilization of this approach in Trinidad, *see* Edwin Carrington, "Industrialization by Invitation in Trinidad," in *Readings in the Political Economy of the Caribbean,* ed. Norman Girvan and Owen Jefferson (Kingston, Jamaica: New World Group Ltd., 1971), pp. 143-50.
13. *British Guiana (Guyana) Development Programme (1966-1972),* Chapter Three, p. 1.
14. Ibid., p. 2.
15. *Second Development Plan 1972-1976,* p. 88. The presentation does add in regard to this proviso that "as a general rule, [it] does not apply to agricultural development" (ibid.).
16. Ibid., pp. 112-13.
17. Ibid., p. 70.
18. Ibid , pp. 72-73.
19. Ibid., p. 184.
20. Ibid., pp. 4-5.
21. Ibid., p. 73.
22. Ibid., p. 51.
23. Ibid., pp. 92-93.
24. Burnham, *A Destiny to Mould* , p. 210.
25. Ibid.
26. "Co-operative Republic Budget 1971, National Assembly of Guyana 4th December 1970" (Georgetown: The Government Printer, n.d.), p. 4.
27. *United Nations, General Assembly, Sixth Special Session* (A/PV. 2215), April 15, 1974, p. 46.
28. "Budget Speech 1969, National Assembly of Guyana, Dr. The Hon. P.A. Reid, Minister of Finance, Friday, 28th February, 1969," Sessional Paper No. 2/69, Second Parliament of Guyana, pp. 5-6.
29 "Budget '74, Co-operative Republic of Guyana, Budget Speech, National Assembly, 10th December, 1973," Sessional Paper No. 2/1973, Third

Parliament of Guyana, p. 6.
30. Forbes Burnham, *Breakthrough: Address by Prime Minister Forbes Burnham, Leader of the People's National Congress, at the 16th Annual Delegates' Congress,* 6th May, 1973 (Georgetown: Guyana Printers, Ltd., n.d.), p. 18.
31. J.J. Villamil, H. Ortiz and E.R. Gutierrez, "Open Systems Planning: A Preliminary Analysis," in *Essays on Race, Economics and Politics in the Caribbean,* ed. Basil Ince (Mayagüez, P.R.: Cuadernos de Arts y Ciencias, Universidad de Puerto Rico, 1972), pp. 71-72.
32. *Second Development Plan, 1972-1976,* p. 70.
33. Ibid., p. 67.
34. Ibid., p. 87.
35. Ibid., p. 113.
36. Ibid., p. 26.
    Norman Girvan has further argued, in an article which helped to set the stage for government takeover of the Aluminum Company of Canada-owned Demerara Bauxite Company in Guyana (and for the more recent takeover of Reynolds Metals Company holdings) as well as moves by the Jamaican government for an enlarged share of revenues from bauxite operations in that country, that "the orientation of technological research reflects the needs of the [North-American controlled bauxite] companies and their parent-country Governments in ways which often diverge from the interests of the Caribbean" (citing examples). He also states that "Conversely, technological research and potentially important for the Caribbean is not undertaken by the companies or is not applied." (Norman Girvan, "Regional Integration vs. Company Integration in the Utilization of Caribbean Bauxite," in *Caribbean Integration: Papers on Social, Political, and Economic Integration,* ed. Sybil Lewis and Thomas G. Mathews, [Rio Piedras, P.R.: Institute of Caribbean Studies, University of Puerto Rico, 1967], p. 112.)
37. *Second Development Plan, 1972-1976,* p. 182.
38. Burnham, *To Own Guyana,* pp. 13-14.
39. Burnham, *Breakthrough,* pp. 13-14.
40. *Lusaka Declaration on Peace, Independence, Development, Cooperation and Democratisation of International Relations and Resolutions of the Third Conference of Heads of State or Government of Non-Aligned Countries* (Lusaka: Ministry of Foreign Affairs, 1970), pp. 25-26.
41. *Main Documents relating to Conference of Non-Aligned Countries from Belgrade, 1961 to Georgetown, 1972* (Georgetown: Ministry of Foreign Affairs, 1972), pp. 123-24.
42. *Documents of the Fourth Conference of Heads of State or Government of Non-Aligned Countries* (Algiers), United Nations General Assembly Document A/9330 (November 22, 1973), p. 69.
43. Ibid., p. 93.
44. Ibid., p. 97.
45. Ibid., p. 95.

46. *British Guiana (Guyana) Development Programme (1966-1972)*, Chapter Six, pp. 1-11.
47. *Second Development Plan, 1972-1976*, pp. 235-37.
    As of November 1973, the University of Guyana's faculty of technology had approximately 250 students studying in the fields of civil, electrical, and mechanical engineering and in architectural and building technology. Assistance had been received from the United Kingdom and Canada in building and equipping technology facilities at the University. (*GUYNEWS* [November 1973], p. 6.)
48. Ptolemy Reid, then minister of finance, in his December 1968 presentation of the 1969 budget to the National Assembly, when discussing technical assistance from abroad and Guyanese counterpart funding for housing, office space, secretarial assistance, and other aspects, commented that "In a number of cases the Government has also been fortunate in securing on a short-term basis, the services of Guyanese specialists who are lecturing or doing research abroad to assist in special assignments of urgent necessity." ("Budget Speech 1969," p. 29.)
    The 1966-72 development plan, in reporting on a 1962 study inventorying vacancies for technically skilled persons, stated that "It should be noted that these estimates were prepared before the political disturbances, which resulted in a considerable amount of emigration among skilled and professional people" (*British Guiana (Guyana) Development Programme (1966-1972)*, Chapter 6, p. 2).
    A Ministry of Information publication stated in August 1971 that approximately 250 Guyanese residents overseas had returned home under the government's re-migration scheme and that the latest group of nineteen included engineers, economists, teachers, geologists, and nurses (*News from Guyana* [Ministry of Information, Georgetown], August 7, 1971, p. 1.)
49. *GUYNEWS*, 2 (July 1973), 4.
50. *Guyana Journal*, 1 (September 1970), 11.
51. Ibid.

Chapter Seven

1. Pablo González-Casanova, "Internal Colonialism and National Development," in *Latin American Radicalism—A Documentary Report on Left and Nationalist Movements,* ed. Irving Louis Horowitz, Josué de Castro, and John Gerassi (New York: Vintage Books, 1969), p. 128 (Originally published in *Studies in Comparative International development.*)
2. *See* in this connection Roy Glasgow, *Guyana: Race and Politics Among Africans and East Indians* (The Hague: Martinus Nijhoff, 1970); J.E. Greene, *Race vs. Politics in Guyana* (Kingston, Jamaica: Institute of Social and Economic Research, University of the West Indies, 1974); and

Robert J. Moore, "Nationalism and Identity in a New World Multi-Racial Society: The Case Study of Guyana," *20th Century Studies* (University of Kent), December 1973.
3. For the differential impact of colonization on the various ethnic groups of Guyana, *see* Raymond T. Smith, *British Guiana* (London: Oxford University Press, 1962), especially pp. 39-51 and 98-143; Smith, *The Negro Family in British Guiana* (London: Routledge and Kegan Paul Ltd., 1956) pp. 191-203 and 221-23; Chandra Jayawardena, *Conflict and Solidarity in a Guianese Plantation* (London: University of London, Athlone Press, 1963), pp. 9-13 and 16-27; and Leo A. Despres, *Cultural Pluralism and Nationalistic Politics in British Guiana* (Chicago: Rand McNally and Co., 1967), pp. 45-67.
4. *See* Walter Rodney, "Masses in Action," in *New World, Guyana Independence Issue* (Georgetown: New World Group Associates, 1966), pp. 30-37.
5. As to the PNC-UDP merger and other aspects of the PNC's development and orientation, *see* Despres, *Cultural Pluralism,* pp. 251-62.
6. The International Commission of Jurists had reported in a study published in late 1965 that Africans were heavily overrepresented, in terms of their percentage of total population, over East Indians in these governmental components. *See Report of the British Guiana Commission of Inquiry: Racial Problems in the Public Service* (Geneva: International Commission of Jurists, 1965), especially Table III, p. 33. Africans had 73.5% of security force positions (a combination, for statistical purposes, of the police and defense forces), compared with 19.9% for East Indians. In the civil service, 53.05% of positions were held by Africans, 33.16% by East Indians. At this time, Africans constituted some 31% of the national population, East Indians approximately 50%.

In its report, the ICJ recommended measures to redress the imbalances and thereafter Burnham declared his government's "willingness to accept these recommendations which are within its power to execute." (*See* statement by Burnham at opening session of the 1965 Constitutional Conference at Lancaster House, London, November 2, 1965, published in Forbes Burnham, *A Destiny to Mould* [London: Longman Caribbean Ltd., 1970], p. 112.) However, it appears that, while some steps were taken toward implementing the ICJ recommendations, Africans continued with numerical (and leadership) domination of the defense and police forces and that the civil service continued to reflect, especially in its upper echelons, African overrepresentation in relation to that ethnic group's proportion of total population.
7. Ronald Segal, *The Race War* (New York: Bantam Books, Inc., 1967), p. 8.
8. James A. Moss, "The Civil Rights Movements and American Foreign Policy," paper presented at symposium on "Conceptual Approaches to the Racial Factor in the International System," Graduate School of International Studies, University of Denver, February 1969, p. 22.
9. George W. Shepherd, Jr. and Tilden J. Lemelle, "Race in the Future of

International Relations," paper prepared for the sixty-sixth annual meeting of the American Political Science Association, Los Angeles, September 1970, p. 10.
10. *Birth of the Co-operative Republic: Speeches by the Prime Minister of Guyana on the Occasion of Guyana Becoming a Republic* (Georgetown: The People's National Congress, n.d.), pp. 43-44.
11. Ibid., pp. 44-45.
12. Ibid., p 46.
13. Ibid., p. 45.
14. *Guyana Graphic,* September 11, 1970, p. 1.
15. *Guyana Graphic,* September 10, 1970, p. 1.
16. *Mirror* (Guyana), September 11, 1970, p. 1; also *Guyana Graphic,* September 11, 1970, p. 1.
17. Typewritten transcript of debate of June 17, 1971, obtained from Parliament Office, pp. 15-17.
18. Cheddi Jagan, *A West Indian State: Pro-Imperialist or Imperialist* (Georgetown: New Guyana Co., Ltd., 1972), p. 50.
19. Mimeographed letter dated May 11, 1971.
20. Forbes Burnham, "Breakthrough: Address by Prime Minister Forbes Burnham, Leader of the People's National Congress, at the 16th Annual Delegates' Congress, 6th May, 1973" (Georgetown: Guyana Printers Ltd., [1973]), p. 33.
21. *Guyana Journal,* Non-Aligned Special Issue (Georgetown: Ministry of External Affairs), 1 (July 1973), 109-110.
22. *GUYNEWS,* 3 (April 1974), 1, 3.
23. Ibid., p. 3.
24. *Sunday Chronicle* (Georgetown), May 26, 1974, p. 1.
25. Paul Singh, "Guyana: Socialism in a Plural Society," in *Fabian Research Series* 307 (London: Fabian Society, October 1972), p. 21.

   For further discussion of Guyana's social system, *see* Pat Robinson, "The Social Structure of Guyana," in *Cooperative Republic: Guyana 1970,* ed. Lloyd Searwar (Georgetown: Ministry of Information and Culture, 1970), pp. 51-76; Raymond Smith, "People and Change", in *New World, Guyana Independence Issue,* pp. 49-54; Elliot P. Skinner, "Social Stratification and Ethnic Identification," in *Peoples and Cultures of the Caribbean,* ed. Michael M. Horowitz, (Garden City: The Natural History Press, [1971?]), pp. 117-32; and Johnson Research Associates (for American University), *Area Handbook for Guyana* (Washington: U.S. Government Printing Office, 1969), p. 67.

   For a consideration of problems of social class analysis in culturally plural societies, *see* Lloyd Braithwaite, "Social Stratification and Cultural Pluralism," in *Peoples and Cultures,* ed. Horowitz, pp. 95-116. For discussion of the "rural proletariat" in Caribbean plantation systems, *see* Sidney Mintz, "The Caribbean Region," *Daedalus* (Spring 1974), pp. 62-63.

26. A.W. Singham and N.L. Singham, "Cultural Domination and Political Subordination: Notes towards a Theory of the Caribbean Political System," *Comparative Studies in Society and History,* 15 (June 1973), pp. 258-88.
27. Ibid., p. 267.
28. Ibid., p. 287.
29. Once Carmichael's essentially "African" approach, under which the best he could offer in Guyana's plural ethnic situation was encouragement for "separate development" of Africans and East Indians, became apparent in his speeches and comments, the Guyanese welcome became less warm, with most groups disassociating themselves from his orientation. *See,* for instance, *Guyana Graphic,* May 6, 1970, reporting that the Ratoon group of intellectuals in Guyana, one of the sponsors of Carmichael's visit, advised that their ideological position must of necessity be different from his.

    For a discussion of the meaning of black power in the Guyanese context, *see* Yereth Knowles, "Guyana, Black Power," in *Guyana: A Composite Monograph,* ed. Brian Irving (Hato Rey, P.R.: Inter American University Press, 1972), pp. 40-47.

    In regard to the black power movement in Trinidad and Tobago and its relationship to the nearly successful revolt of April 1970, *see* Frank MacDonald, "The Commonwealth Caribbean," in *The United States and the Caribbean,* ed. Tad Szulc (Englewood Cliffs, N.J.: Prentice-Hall, Inc., 1971), especially pp. 154-56.
30. L.F.S. Burnham, "Towards a Co-Operative Republic," Address to 12th Annual Delegates' Congress [PNC], Georgetown, April 6, 1969 (Georgetown: People's National Congress, n.d.), p. 10.
31. *Policy for the New Co-op Republic,* The 13th Annual Conference of the People's National Congress, Queen's College, April 2-8, 1970 (Georgetown: The Daily Chronicle Ltd., n.d.), p. 20.
32. Speech of February 24, 1970, as reported in *Birth of the Cooperative Republic of Guyana,* pp. 42-43.
33. Speech of February 23, 1970, as reported in *Birth of the Cooperative Republic of Guyana,* pp. 28, 30.
34. Speech of April 13, 1970, as reported in *Guyana Journal,* 1 (September 1970), 6.
35. Ibid. Relationships between youth discontents and black power movements are considered in Knowles' essay "Guyana, Black Power," *Guyana: A Composite Monograph,* ed. Irving, p. 42.
36. Speech of February 23, 1970, as reported in *Guyana Journal,* 1 (September 1970), 6.
37. *Guyana Journal,* Non-Aligned Special Issue, 1 (July 1973), 114-15.
38. David Lowenthal, *West Indian Societies* (New York: Oxford University Press, 1972), p. 245.
39. Ibid.

40. My understanding from personal interviews in Georgetown is that the continuing absence of television is based, at least in part, on an intentional decision of governmental leaders to avoid the external influences it would bring.
41. Gordon K. Lewis, *The Growth of the Modern West Indies* (London: MacGibbon and Kee Ltd., 1968), p. 258.
42. Ibid.
43. Ibid. As to another element of continuing influence from the Dutch period, namely in the land law system, *see* Fenton H.W. Ramsahoye, *The Development of Land Law in British Guiana* (Dobbs Ferry, N.Y.: Oceana Publications, Inc., 1966).
44. For a critical commentary on Theatre Guild offerings, *see* W.A. McAndrew, "Drama in Trouble," *The Sunday Chronicle* First Anniversary Supplement, May 28, 1967, p. 41.

   For background on the Theatre Guild and discussion of its choice of productions—which admittedly included some Guyanese and West Indian plays—*see* Frank Pilgrim, "Drama in Guyana," *Kaie* (official publication of the National History and Arts Council of Guyana), Special Expo '67 Issue, No. 4 (July 1967), pp. 35-36.

   Cheddi Jagan's view regarding the local drama scene was: "Even the Theatre Guild, who, in the past, have been putting on some very interesting plays with a local touch, have ceased doing this since the Americans forced their way on the scene. A lot of foreign hog-wash is being presented now. The Guyanese society is now being indoctrinated" (*Evening Post* [Georgetown], May 22, 1967, p. 8).
45. *See* in this connection comments regarding education and other aspects of socialization in the West Indies in E.J.B. Rose and associates, *Colour and Citizenship: A Report on British Race Relations* (London: Oxford University Press, 1969), pp. 420-21.
46. Good Friday, Holy Saturday, Easter Monday, and Christmas (*Guyana Year Book, 1966* [Georgetown: Guyana Graphic, Ltd., n.d.], p. 3).
47. Among the better known and mostly London-based Guyanese writers and artists working abroad as of independence were painters Denis Williams and Aubrey Williams (unrelated) and writers Jan Carew, E.R. Braithwaite, and Wilson Harris. However, poets A.J. Seymour and Martin Carter and playwright Norman E. Cameron had remained in Guyana. Seymour has been a mainstay of the local cultural establishment, especially in his work with the National History and Arts Council and activities related to conferences of writers and artists. Carter served for several years in the Burnham government cabinet as Minister of Information. Cameron, generally acknowledged to be Guyana's first author of dramas, has through the years been prolific in producing essays, works of historical interpretation including a pathbreaking two-volume work, *The Evolution of the Negro,* and political commentary. His *Guyanese Library and Its Impact,* first published in the *Sunday Chronicle* from February 2 to May 25, 1969, then published (1971) in pamphlet form by the author, is a

valuable commentary and bibliography regarding books by Guyanese authors.
48. From summary of remarks of May 30, 1966, as published in *Kaie*, No. 3 (December 1966), p. 3.
49. Ibid.

    The noted West Indian writer and political activist C.L.R. James also called for the establishment of an independent publishing house at approximately the same time. *See* "Tomorrow and Today: A Vision," in *New World—Guyana Independence Issue*, p. 89.
50. *Kaie*, No. 3 (December 1966), pp. 3-4.
51. *Birth of the Cooperative Republic*, p. 38.
52. Ibid.
53. Ibid., pp. 39-40.
54. Hindu days observed commemorate Phagwah and Deepavali, Muslim, Eid-ul-Ahza and Youman Naubi. Eight other holidays are observed, namely New Year, Republic Day, Good Friday, Easter Monday, Labour Day, Commonwealth Day, Christmas, and Boxing Day (*Guyana Year Book 1967* [Georgetown: Guyana Graphic Ltd., n.d.], p. 3).

    The statement is sometimes made that as a result of the new schedule each of the major religions has two of its major festivals commemorated. While this is true, four holidays relate to or are chronologically contiguous with Christian events—Good Friday, Easter Monday, Christmas, and Boxing Day (December 26)—while only two holidays relate to Hindu, and two to Muslim, observances.
55. In this connection, *see Action Radio Times* (Georgetown: Guyana Broadcasting Service), 1 (October 1969), 2.
56. *Guyana Graphic*, September 27, 1974, p. 1.

    A modern printing establishment, Guyana Printers Ltd., was established by the government in connection with resumption of publication of the *Chronicle* on a daily basis. The *Graphic* was merged into the *Chronicle*.
57. *See* for instance *Our First Village*, adapted from a story by R.A. Dowden, illustrated by H.A. Bascom (Georgetown: Ministry of Education, 1972); *They Came from Africa* (one of a series), written by Barbara Greaves, illustrated by Tom Feelings, introduction and text for adults by Iyaluua Adams (Georgetown: Ministry of Education, 1972); and *Farmer Smith*, written by Sibil Cort, illustrated by Angold Thompson (Georgetown: Ministry of Education, 1973).
58. Amongst the noteworthy titles, in this connection, are Lloyd Searwar, ed., *Cooperative Republic—Guyana 1970* (Georgetown: Ministry of Information and Culture, 1970); A.J. Seymour, ed., *New Writing in the Caribbean* (Georgetown: Guyana Lithographic Co. Ltd., 1972); Donald A.B. Trotman, *Guyana and the World* (Georgetown: United Nations Association of Guyana, 1973); and *A New Guyana* (Georgetown: Ministry of Information, Culture and Youth, [1973?]).

59. *GUYNEWS*, 3 (February 1974), 8. Previously, Guyana Information Service Films, a unit of the Ministry of Information, Culture and Youth, had produced a 35mm film of feature length (100 minutes) and of considerable sophistication based upon the 1972 Caribbean Festival of Creative Arts held in Guyana. University of Guyana historian Robert Moore provided the film's written framework and a young Guyanese filmmaker, Brian Stuart-Young, acted as producer-director. A description of the film, "World of the Caribbean," issued by the Ministry of Information, states that it was viewed as the first significant step in establishment of a local film industry and asserts that "The Government of Guyana recognises the importance of developing such an industry because, like other third world states, it sees the need for films which reflect accurately the local and regional environment and in which the people can identify their way of life" (mimeographed release captioned "World of the Caribbean," p. 1).
60. *Mirror*, January 22, 1970, p. 8.
61. *Mirror*, December 1, 1970, p. 1.
62. Janet Jagan, *Army Intervention in the 1973 Elections in Guyana* (Georgetown: PPP Education Committee, 1973), p. 52.
63. *Facts on File*, Vol. 33, material for April 22-28, 1973, p. 330.
64. Cited in Jagan, *Army Intervention*, p. 52.
65. The 1966 conference in Georgetown was apparently the first major meeting of writers and artists of the Commonwealth Caribbean. Guyanese poet A.J. Seymour, conference chairman, has noted that there were discussions regarding the holding of such a meeting in connection with Trinidad and Tobago's independence in 1962. "This unfortunately did not materialize," Seymour comments, "and it fell to Guyana's Prime Minister to inaugurate the Conference under discussion" (A.J. Seymour, "Reflections on the Conference," *Kaie* (December 1966), p. 9).
66. *Documents of the Fourth Conference of Heads of State or Government of Non-Aligned Countries* (Algiers), issued as United Nations General Assembly Document A/9330, 22 November 1973, pp. 73-74.
67. Ibid., p. 88.
68. Harold Lutchman, Epilogue, in *Middle Class Colonial Politics: A Study of Guyana with Special Reference to the Period 1920-1931*, Diss. University of Manchester 1967, p. 298.
69. Ibid., pp. 298-99. *See also* Lutchman *From Colonialism to Crown Colony: Aspects of Political Development in Guyana*, (Rio Piedras, Puerto Rico: Institute of Caribbean Studies, University of Puerto Rico, 1974), especially pp. 213 and following.
70. Smith, *British Guiana*, pp. 168-69. *See* in regard to external ideological influences on development of the People's Progressive Party Despres, *Cultural Pluralism*, pp. 178-92, and Ernst Halperin, "Racism and Communism in British Guiana," *Journal of the Inter-American Studies*, 7 (January 1965), especially pp. 106-21.
71. Despres, *Cultural Pluralism*, p. 255.
72. Ibid., p. 7.

73. Charles C. Moskos, Jr., *The Sociology of Political Independence: A Study of Nationalist Attitudes among West Indian Leaders* (Cambridge, Mass: Schenkman Publishing Co., 1967), pp. 20-21.
74. Glasgow, Guyana; *Race and Politics,* p. 140.
75. Lewis, *The Growth of the Modern West Indies,* p. 285. Lewis is no less critical of the People's National Congress and United Force parties, referring to their "conscious exploitation of race" and "basic opportunism" (ibid.).
76. Burnham, *A Destiny to Mould,* pp. 153, 157-58.
77. It was several years before Michael Manley's approach to socialism emerged in Jamaica.

    In terms of comparative political cultures in the Commonwealth Caribbean, Charles Moskos had found in a series of interviews of West Indian leaders conducted in 1961-62 (Guyana, Jamaica, Trinidad, Barbados, Dominica, and Grenada were the polities included in the survey) that Guyana was highest on a scale of "egalitarian" attitudes. *See* Charles C. Moskos, Jr. and Wendell Bell, "Attitudes Toward Equality," in *The Democratic Revolution in the West Indies,* ed. Wendell Bell (Cambridge, Mass.: Schenkman Publishing Co., 1967), p. 103. The methodology employed is discussed in Moskos, *The Sociology of Political Independence,* pp. 96-105. It should be considered in evaluating these finding, however, that there were only thirteen leaders in the Guyanese sample.
78. "Introduction: The Anatomy of African Socialism," in *African Socialism* ed. William H. Friedland and Carl G. Rosberg, Jr (Stanford: Stanford University Press, 1964), p. 9.
79. Burnham, *A Destiny to Mould,* p. 152.
80. Ibid., pp. 200-201.
81. Speech to People's National Congress Regional Conference, Georgetown, August 24, 1969, in Burnham, *A Destiny to Mould,* pp. 156, 158-59.
82. "The Concept of the Co-operative Republic," text of address by Mrs. Shirley Patterson, Minister of Education, during the National Assembly debate August 29, 1969, pp. 10-11 (mimeographed document). Mrs. Patterson was later remarried (to Hamilton Green, a key figure in Burnham's cabinets) and uses her maiden name, Field-Ridley, in public life.
83. Eusi Kwayana, "Economic Relations in Pre-Republican Guyana," in *Co-op Republic: Guyana 1970,* ed. Searwar, p. 198.
84. *Policy for the New Co-Op Republic,* pp. 13, 23
85. *To Own Guyana,* Address by Prime Minister Forbes Burnham, Leader of the People's National Congress, at the 14th Annual Delegates' Congress of the Party, 18th April 1971 (Georgetown: P.N.C., n.d.), p. 51.
86. *Main Documents Relating to Conferences of Non-Aligned Countries from Belgrade, 1961 to Georgetown, 1972* (Georgetown: Ministry of Foreign Affairs, 1972), p. 118.
87. *Breakthrough,* address by Forbes Burnham of May 6, 1973, p. 31.
88. Paul Singh, "Guyana: Socialism in a Plural Society," in *Fabian Research Series* 307 (London: Fabian Society, October 1972), p. 19.

89. Harold A. Lutchman, "The Co-operative Republic of Guyana," *Caribbean Studies*, 10 (October 1970), 114. *See also* Lutchman's "Some Administrative Problems of the Co-operative Republic of Guyana," *Journal of Administration Overseas*, 10 (April 1971), 87-99.
90. Dr. Cheddi Jagan, "Our People Deserve a Better Future," speech in the National Assembly February 23, 1970 (Georgetown: New Guyana Co., [1970]), p. 2.
91. Cheddi Jagan, *The West on Trial: The Fight for Guyana's Freedom* (Berlin, German Democratic Republic: Seven Seas Publishers, 1972), p. 398.
92. Ibid., p. 416.
93. Cheddi Jagan, *A West Indian State: Pro-Imperialist or Anti-Imperialist* (Georgetown: New Guyana Co., 1972), pp. 56-57.
94. "The Caribbean Revolution—Tasks and Perspectives," opening address by Dr. Cheddi Jagan, General Secretary of the People's Progressive Party, to the Caribbean Anti-imperialist Conference held in Georgetown, Guyana, South America, August 30-31, 1972 (Georgetown: Secretariat of the Caribbean Anti-imperialist Conference, Freedom House, n.d.), p. 8 (mimeographed document).
95. Ibid., p. 7.
96. *See* in this connection the concluding portion of chapter two, "Political Leadership for the New Nation." For a summary of Burnham's "Declaration of Sophia" speech before a special congress of the PNC on the tenth anniversary of his premiership and of the PNC in government, see *Keesing's Contemporary Archives*, October 1, 1976, p. 27971.
97. *GIS News* (Ministry of Information and Culture, Georgetown), May 3, 1976.
98. *GIS News*, May 4, 1976.

Index

Action Programme for Economic Cooperation, 14, 66, 68, 82, 110, 111
Africa, 2, 3, 4, 9, 19, 23, 56, 60, 67, 90, 91, 92, 101
African, 1, 2, 3, 4, 7, 85-88, 107, 115, 116
African Liberation Day, 92
African Society for Cultural Relations with Independent Africa, 89
Afro-Asian, 59
Agriculture, 25, 32, 51, 54, 56, 75, 82
Algeria, 67
Algiers, 14, 67, 68, 82, 102-103
Aluminum Company of Canada (ALCAN), 10, 13, 64-65, 78
Americans, 10, 30, 56, 58, 73, 105
Amerindians, 1, 2, 12, 45, 46, 51-54, 70, 91, 93
Anglo-Dutch War of 1781, 3
Angola, 70
Antigua, 28, 31
Anti-Trust, 65
Arbitration (Borders), 41, 42, 44, 47
Argentina, 66
Asia, 67, 88, 91, 101
Atkinson Field, 60
Australia, 30
Autonomy, 63
Azores, 4

Bandung, 88
Banking, 10, 12, 13, 17, 72, 73
Barbados, 2, 4, 10, 28, 29, 31, 32, 33, 69, 71, 83, 99

Barrow, Maurice, 64
Barrow, Errol, 28
Bartica, 2
Bauxite, 2, 10, 13, 26, 54, 64, 65, 67, 69, 79, 111
Beard, Charles, 21
Belgrade, 68
Belize, 29
Benn, Brindley, 24
Berbice, 1, 3, 12, 20, 63
Berbice River, 2
Best, Lloyd, 99
Bhagwan, Moses, 24
Bolivia, 66
Booker McConnell, Ltd., 13, 24, 26, 65
Bookers' Guiana, 10
Border Disputes, 41-45, 48-50, 51, 53, 54, 71
Brazilia, 44
Brazil, 2, 7, 12, 44-45, 53, 54, 66, 68, 69, 70, 91
Brewster, Havelock, 34
British, 1, 2, 4, 6, 8, 9, 19, 30, 36-37, 41, 42-43, 56-57, 58, 63-64, 85-86, 105
British Guiana, 2, 5, 10, 28, 30, 31, 42-43, 44, 56
British Guiana Constitution Committee, 6
British Home Office, 12
Burnham, Forbes, 1, 6, 7, 8, 9, 10, 12, 14, 15, 17, 19-20, 22, 23, 25, 26-27, 28, 29-30, 31, 33, 34, 36-37, 38-39,

43, 44, 45, 46, 50-51, 52, 53, 56-64, 68-71, 73, 76, 78, 79-81, 83, 86, 89-91, 92-94, 96-98, 100-101, 102, 104, 105, 106-108, 109, 110-111, 113, 115, 116

Cairo, 68
Caldera, Rafael, 48
Calvani, Aristides, 35, 46, 48
Canada, 30, 61, 64, 65, 72, 87, 93, 99
Canadian-West-Indian Trade Agreement, 64
Cape Verde, 4
Capitalism, 24-26, 71, 105, 110, 112
Caracas, 11, 35, 49, 52
Caribbean, 2, 3, 10, 28, 29, 36, 70, 87, 89, 90, 97, 98, 100, 101, 113
    Anti-Imperialist Conference, 113
    Community (CARICOM), 10, 29, 33, 34
    Development Bank, 10, 29
    Free Trade Area (CARIFTA), 10, 28, 29, 31, 32, 33, 34, 37, 76
Carmichael, Stokely, 95
Carter, Jimmy, 70
Castro, Fidel, 8, 55, 68, 69
Central Intelligence Agency (CIA), 7, 57, 112
Chaguaramas, 10
Chang, Arthur, 13
Cheeks, R.E., 52
Chiang Kai-Shek, 61
China, 1, 2, 3, 4, 61, 68, 69, 70, 73, 86, 88, 116
Coalition Government, 9, 32, 47, 55, 57, 58, 59, 60, 62, 68, 71, 86, 88
Coastal Area, 1, 51, 99
Cold War, 6, 7, 106
Colombia, 66
Colonialism, 6, 24, 39, 85, 103, 104, 105, 109, 112
Colonization, 1, 85, 86, 99
Commonwealth Caribbean, 10, 16, 22, 28, 29, 34, 36, 37, 45, 55, 64, 67, 68, 69, 72, 74, 83, 87, 94, 95, 102, 105, 106, 115
Communications, 37, 75, 103
Communism, 6, 7, 8, 24, 25, 56, 65, 68, 70, 73, 75, 82, 87, 104, 109, 112, 113
Congress of Industrial Organizations, 21
Constitution, 5-10, 11, 14, 25, 37, 52, 62, 63
Cooperative National Bank, 12, 101
Cooperative Republic, 3, 5, 12, 13, 32, 52, 63, 74, 89, 91, 108, 109, 116
Corentyne River, 42, 43, 44
Cuba, 7-8, 55-56, 61, 66, 69, 70, 71, 102, 116
Cuffy, 3, 12, 63-64
Culture, 43, 44, 85, 86, 87, 89, 95, 99-103, 105, 114
Cuyuni River, 2
Czechoslovakia, 69

d'Aguiar, Peter, 7-9, 19, 22-23, 46, 101, 105
Daly, Vere T., 4, 6, 8
Dar es Salaam, 66
Da Silva, Eleanor, 16
Davies, Nathaniel, 65
Decolonization, 1, 35, 37, 45, 87
De Gaulle, Charles, 62
Demas, William, 72
Demerara, 2, 3
Demerara Bauxite Company (DEMBA), 13, 65, 67, 78
Demerara River, 2, 3
Demilitarization, 13, 43, 44
Democracy, 58, 59, 107, 109
Depression, 5
Despres, Leo, 6, 105
Developing Nations, 10, 25, 33, 59, 60, 66, 67, 68, 76, 77, 78, 81, 82, 83, 92, 98, 99, 103
Development Plans
    1966-72: 72-76, 78, 83
    1972-76: 55, 72-76, 78-80, 83
Diamonds, 50

Index   155

District System, 8
Dominica, 83
Duggal, Ved, 72
Duncan, Philip, 93
Dutch, 1, 2, 3, 4, 41, 42, 43, 99, 102
Dutch West Indies Company, 2

East Africa, 68
East India, 1, 2, 4, 5, 7, 8, 20, 23, 85, 86, 87, 111
Economic Development, 4, 10, 13, 14, 17, 25, 29, 31-35, 43-45, 55-56, 60, 62, 65, 66, 67, 72, 73-75, 76-77, 79-82, 96, 97, 98, 101, 102, 103, 105, 107, 110
Ecuador, 66
Education, 5, 67, 83, 94-95
El Dorado, 2
Essequibo River, 2, 3, 10, 41, 46
Ethnic Groups, 7, 8, 34, 59, 85, 86-89, 91, 114, 115, 116
External Trade Bureau, 76

Fishing, 69
Food, 74-75, 80
Ford, Gerald, 70
Foreign Investors, 37, 45, 49, 73-74, 79-80
Foreign Policy, 10, 28, 32, 56, 57, 60-62, 70-71, 75-77, 91-92
France, 61
Franchise, 5
French, 2, 3, 102
Freyre, Gilberto, 45
Friedland, William, 107

General Assembly, 11, 37, 49, 66, 77, 82
Geneva, 42, 48, 49
Georgetown, 3, 7, 10, 11, 12, 15, 20, 21, 22, 23, 29, 43, 44, 46, 49, 52, 53, 60, 65, 66, 67, 68, 69, 81, 83, 92, 93, 102, 110, 111, 113
Georgetown Declaration, 14
German Democratic Republic, 55, 69

Giniger, Henry, 12
Gonzalez-Casanova, Pablo, 85
Gordon, Lincoln, 59
Great Britain, 3, 15, 16, 41, 42, 44, 58, 61, 64, 68, 72, 99, 100, 102
Greene, J.E., 23
Grenada Declaration, 30, 32, 38, 115
Guevara, Ernesto (Che), 55
Guiana Agricultural Workers Union, 8
Gutierrez, E.R., 78
Guyana
    Broadcasting Service, 101
    Defense Force, 44, 53, 54, 116
    Labour Union, 20
    Liberator Party, 14, 16, 23
    National Cooperative Bank, 97
    United Muslim Party, 11

Haiti, 3, 102
Havana, 11, 69
Health, 5, 22
Henfrey, Colin, 3
Hindu, 48
Hope, Frank, 78
Housing, 10, 22, 74, 75, 80
Hungary, 69
Hydroelectric Power, 54, 55, 69, 82

Ideologies, 5, 7, 24, 25, 26, 38, 85, 86, 87, 95, 102, 103, 105, 108, 109, 112, 113, 114
Ince, Basil, 41, 71
Independence, 1, 7-11, 13, 17, 26, 28, 36, 39, 41, 42, 43, 44, 47, 50, 52, 54, 59, 60, 62, 63, 69-72, 75, 82, 86, 93, 96, 97, 98, 101, 102, 104, 107, 109, 114, 115
India, 4, 6, 20, 67, 104
Indian, 3, 4, 8, 10
Indian Political Revolutionary Associates, 24
Industrialization, 14, 36, 54, 56, 68, 74, 75, 79-80, 81, 98, 108
Institute of Race Relations, 12

156 Guyana Emergent

Inter-American Development Bank, 35
Interior Development Committee, 51
International Bauxite Association, 76

Jack, Hubert, 50, 66
Jagan, Cheddi, 1, 5-9, 12, 17-23, 24, 25, 26, 30, 31, 39, 46, 47, 55-56, 58, 59, 60, 61-62, 70, 86, 87, 102, 104, 105, 111-112, 113, 114, 116
Jagan, Cheddi, Jr., 22, 64
Jagan, Janet, 5, 6, 21, 22, 87
Jamaica, 5, 11, 15, 32, 39, 66, 68, 71, 98, 99, 102
John, Llewellyn, 14
Johnson, Lyndon, 59
Josephson, Matthew, 21

Kennedy, John F., 24, 56
King, Kenneth, 17
King, Sidney, 7 (see also Kwayana, Eusi)
Kingston, 11, 102
Kwayana, Eusi, 7, 19, 23, 109
Kyk-over-al, 2

Labor, 3, 7, 10, 22, 77, 79, 81, 105
Lands Commission, 52
Latin America, 14, 46, 67, 91, 113
Legislative Council, 4, 5, 6, 22, 28, 30, 31
Le Melle, Tilden, 88
Lenin, 6, 24, 25, 111, 114, 116
Lewis, W. Arthur, 72
Lewis, Gordon, 99, 105-106
Linden, 2, 54
London, 8, 11, 19, 43, 49, 56, 57, 68
Lord Moyne, 5
Lowenthal, David, 99
Lusaka, 11, 14, 66, 76, 81, 91, 109
Lutchman, Harold, 103-104, 111

Madeira, 3
Magdalenenberg, 64

Maha Sabha, 48
Makouria, 61
Malaysia, 53
Mallet-Prevost, Severe, 41
Malta, 4
Manley, Michael, 68
Manpower Citizens Association, 8
Marx, 6, 21, 24, 25, 114
Marxism, 41, 104, 106, 111, 113, 114, 116
Mazaruni River, 2, 54, 69
Mentus, Ric, 15
Mexico, 66, 102
Mingo, Vibert, 70
Mining, 13, 53
Mitchell, Sir Harold, 7-8
Monserrat, 29, 83
Montreal, 64
Moscow, 24, 113
Moskos, Charles, 105
Moss, James, 88
Moyne Commission, 5
Multinationals, 13

Narain, Sase, 48
Nath, Dwarka, 4
National Assembly, 13, 14, 16, 22, 23, 31, 47, 48, 52, 53, 62, 63, 68, 76, 91, 97, 101, 108, 112
Nationalism, 113
Nationalization, 5, 13, 24, 26, 65, 67, 71, 111, 116
National Service Program, 51
Nehru, 21, 22
Netherlands, 3, 43
Neutralism, 60, 71, 107
New Amsterdam, 11
New Delhi, 11, 66
Newman, Peter, 2
New River, 10, 42, 43
New York, 3, 11, 67
Nicholson, H.H., 7
Non-Aligned Nations, 14, 28, 55, 61, 62, 66, 67, 76, 77, 79, 82, 91, 92, 98, 102, 103, 109, 110, 111, 113

Index 157

North Atlantic Treaty Organization, 94
Nyerere, Julius, 91

Oil, 17, 55, 67
Orinoco River, 8
Ortiz, H., 78
Ottawa, 11

Paramaribo, 11, 43
Parties, Political, 5-9, 11, 14, 15, 16, 17, 22-25, 38, 47, 48, 63, 64, 106
Partition, 7, 23
Patterson, Shirley, 108
Peace Corps, 112
Peking, 11, 68
Pengel, Johannes, 43
People's National Movement (PNM), 6, 95
People's National Congress (PNC), 6, 7, 9, 11, 14, 16, 17, 22-26, 29, 31, 33, 39, 46, 47, 55, 58, 59, 62, 63, 68, 71, 78-81, 86, 87, 91, 92, 102, 105, 106, 109-111, 112-116
People's Progressive Party (PPP), 6-9, 11, 14-17, 22, 23, 24, 25, 26, 31, 39, 47, 48, 55, 58, 59, 63, 68, 69, 70, 71, 86, 87, 91, 101, 102, 104, 105-106, 112, 113, 115-116
Peru, 66, 69
Poland, 69
Polarization, 87, 88, 106
Political Affairs Committee, 20, 21, 22
Pomeroon, 12
Port Mourant, 20
Portuguese, 1, 2, 3, 4, 7, 85, 86, 93, 105
Preiswerk, Roy, 55
Proportional Representation, 9, 15, 57
Public Service International, 57
Puerto Rico, 89

Racism, 21, 48, 64, 85, 93, 96
Radosh, Ronald, 57

Ramphal, S.S., 30, 39, 44, 45, 49, 65, 77
Regional Unity, 10, 28, 30, 32, 33, 34, 35, 38, 59, 98
Reid, Ptolemy, 76, 77-78
Resources, 13, 25, 26, 32, 33, 36, 39, 44, 45, 49, 50, 60, 66, 67, 68, 70, 71, 72, 74, 76, 78, 79, 81, 82, 83, 94, 108, 109, 110
Reynolds Metals, 10, 13, 26, 65
Rhodesia, 58, 93
Rio de Janeiro, 11, 44
Rivers, 2, 42-43, 50, 53
Robertson, Sir James, 6
Rodney, Walter, 24
Rosberg, Carl, 107
Rupununi, 12, 45, 50, 51, 52, 115
Rusk, Dean, 56
Russia, 41, 42, 55, 61, 69, 70, 71, 88, 104, 109, 116

Salazar, 105
Sandys, Duncan, 8-9
Sawmill Workers' Union, 22
Schlesinger, Arthur, Jr., 56, 57
Schumacher, E.F., 78
Security Council, 61
Sedney, Dr. Jules, 13, 43, 44
Segal, Aaron, 33-34
Segal, Ronald, 88
Seldes, George, 21
Shepherd, George, 88
Shipping, 4, 10, 13, 49
Singh, Benedit, 23
Singh, David, 68
Singh, Feilden, 16, 19, 22, 23
Singh, Paul, 94, 111
Singh, Rickey, 16
Singham, Archibald, 94-95
Singham, N.L., 94-95
Slave Revolts, 3, 12, 63
Slaves, 1-4, 19, 51, 85, 98, 99
Smith, Ian, 58
Smith, Raymond, 4, 6
Socialism, 6, 12, 21, 25-27, 32, 38, 62,

71, 82, 86, 107-109, 110, 111, 112, 113, 116
Society for Racial Equality, 7, 23
South Africa, 88, 89, 91, 92, 93
Spanish, 2, 41
Sri Lanka, 14
Stabroek, 3
Sugar, 2, 3, 8, 10, 13, 17, 19, 20, 69, 72, 99
Surinam, 3, 10, 13, 41, 42-46, 70

Tanzania, 66
Taxes, 2, 7, 29, 73
Technology, 34, 67, 72, 73, 76, 77-84
Third World, 76, 83, 87
Thomas, Clive, 24, 34, 39, 71
Thomas, J. Henry, 61
Thompson, P.S., 66
Tobago, 29, 32, 35, 36, 66, 69, 83, 87, 96
Trade, 14, 34, 62, 67, 68, 71, 72, 76-77
Trade Unions, 5, 48, 57
Transport, 67, 68, 75, 77
Trinidad, 6, 10, 16, 19, 28, 32, 34, 35, 36, 39, 43, 48, 64, 66, 69, 71, 83, 87, 95, 96, 99
Tumatumari, 54

Unemployment, 5, 80, 81
Unilever, 31
Unions, 7, 8
United Democratic Party (UDP), 86
United Force (UF), 11, 12, 14, 16, 19, 22, 23, 25, 31, 32, 47, 52, 55, 58, 59, 62, 63, 71, 86, 87, 91, 102, 105, 106
United Nations, 10, 11, 37, 41, 42, 49, 59, 61, 66, 67, 72, 77, 82, 104
United States, 4, 7, 8, 12, 13, 20, 21, 47, 48, 56, 57, 59, 60, 61, 62, 64, 65, 69, 70, 71, 72, 86, 87, 89, 90, 93, 95, 99, 101, 102, 104, 109, 112
University of Guyana, 45, 94, 111
Uruguay, 66

Venezuela, 2, 7, 10, 12, 13, 34, 35, 41, 42-49, 51, 52, 54, 66, 70, 91
Villamil, J.J., 78

Waddell, D.A.G., 64
Wagner Act, 7
Washington, 11, 56, 57, 61, 70, 107
West Indians, 4, 5, 28, 29, 30, 31, 33-34, 64, 83, 97, 99, 101
West Indies Federation, 10, 30, 31, 39
Williams, Dr. Eric, 6, 19, 35
Wizmar-MacKenzie, 2
Working People's Alliance (WPA), 19, 23, 24, 116
Working People's Vanguard Party (WPVP), 24
World Bank, 56

Yugoslavia, 61, 67, 69

Zambia, 66
Zander, Arnold, 57-58

About the Author

Born in Albany, New York, April 22, 1927, Robert H. Manley has been a member of the Department of Political Science at Seton Hall University since September 1973, currently serving as an Associate Professor. Previously, he taught political science at the Atlanta University Center, where he was Director of the Non-Western Studies Program, the City University of New York and the University of Puerto Rico, where for three years he was a research associate with the Institute of Caribbean Studies. He recieved the B.A. from Colgate, the M.P.A. from Harvard, the J.D. from Cornell, and the Ph.D. from SUNY Albany. His educational background also includes work at the University of Manchester, England on a Rotary Foundation Fellowship and with the Center for Studies in International Law and International Relations of the Hague Academy of International Law on a grant from the Academy. Founding editor of the journal, *International and Comparative Public Policy,* and a contributor to scholarly publications in the fields of public policy, law, and Caribbean studies, he is a member of the New York and New Jersey bars.